"A priceless heritage":

A history *of*
Heritage College *and* Seminary
in three essays

Michael A.G. Haykin *and* Jonathan N. Cleland

BLESS THY WORD

Bless Thy Word, O Lord we pray;
Make it real to us this day.
Set our hearts with love afire,
Kindled, burning with desire
That we may the Saviour see
In His power and majesty:
Hear His voice in every line
And the glory all be Thine.

As we meet with one accord,
Eyes of faith upon the Lord,
Rest on us; Thy Spirit seal;
Fill us with a holy zeal.
Set us free from every sin;
Reign supreme, yea reign within.
Lord of life we crown Thee now,
King of Kings before Thee bow;
Evermore to sing Thy praise,
Live for Thee through endless days.

Paul Holliday

To the faculty, staff, students, and board members of
Central Baptist Seminary (1949–1993),
London Baptist Bible College & Seminary (1976–1993),
and Heritage College & Seminary (1993–2023).

"*A priceless heritage*": *A history of Heritage College and Seminary in three essays*
Michael A.G. Haykin and Jonathan N. Cleland

© 2023 Heritage Seminary Press,
Heritage College and Seminary
175 Holiday Inn Drive
Cambridge, ON
Canada
N3C 3T2.

eBook: 978-1-77484-142-6
Paperback: 978-1-77484-141-9

Contents

Foreword		11
1	"Great is Thy faithfulness": A history of Central Baptist Seminary, 1949-1993	15
2	"Truth aflame": A history of London Baptist Bible College and Seminary, 1976–1993	61
3	"An enterprise of faith": A history of Heritage Baptist College and Theological Seminary, 1993–2023	93

Foreword

This book came about in part as the result of a phone call that Michael had with Jon in the fall of 2022. They had just finished writing the history of West Highland Baptist Church in Hamilton, Ontario, and as they concluded that book, Jon asked Michael if there was any plan to write the history of Heritage, for the thirtieth anniversary of its founding was just around the corner in 2023. Twelve months later, they are thankful to God and his grace in allowing them to pen this project together. Michael wrote the initial draft of Chapter 1 and Jon drew up the first drafts of Chapters 2 and 3. Michael then edited Chapters 2 and 3 fairly extensively and Jon did the same for Chapter 1. The three essays are thus very much a joint project.

Michael and Jon are thankful for a number of people without whose aid this book would not have been possible. Over the past thirty years, Michael has had interviews or conversations with a good number of people whose insight into the history of Central has been important for the writing of Chapter 1. He is deeply grateful to Edith McCredie, Hal MacBain, Charlie Tipp, Bob Holmes, Sid Kerr, Ted Angrove—all of whom are now with the Lord—as well as Marina Coldwell, Jack Hannah, Richard Long, Richard Mitchell, and Rene McCaugherty Simpson for answering his questions and providing needed perspectives. Marina Coldwell's personal archive of material relating to the history of Central, London, and Heritage has been absolutely invaluable. Without those resources that she had preserved, it would have been extremely challenging indeed to have written the history of Central. Those resources are now in the Archives of Heritage College and Seminary, Cambridge, Ontario.

Informal conversations that Jon had with Dave Barker, Stan Fowler, and Mike Anderson about the history of London and Heritage were a vital foundation for Chapters 2 and 3. He is also thankful to Gerry and Liz Benn, Marvin Brubacher, Theresa Beach, Sylvia Chin, and Rick Reed, for being willing to be interviewed and answer various questions. A big thank-you also to Dave Barker, Marvin Brubacher, Gerry and Liz Benn, Mike Anderson, Theresa Beach, and Laura Cleland for their comments on the initial drafts of Chapters 2 and 3. Heather Okrafka, Carolyn Burgess, Shawn Goble, and Steve Jones provided invaluable details about Heritage and the Fellowship of Evangelical Baptist Churches in Canada.

Finally, both Michael and Jon are deeply grateful to those students who contributed their testimonies and stories to these historical essays.

Without being hagiographical, the authors have sought to be gracious and historically accurate in their treatment of the histories of Central, London, and Heritage. Our three essays are a highly selective narrative, but one, we believe, that presents the theological identities of, and traces the major events of, all three schools. These are stories that needed to be written, and we hope that this book records a slice of Canadian church history that both glorifies the Triune God and edifies those who read it.

> Michael A.G. Haykin & Jonathan N. Cleland
> All Saints' Eve/Reformation Day, 2023

1

"Great is Thy faithfulness": A history of Central Baptist Seminary, 1949-1993

As 1981 drew to a close, Michael Haykin was on the verge of graduating from the University of Toronto and Wycliffe College with his doctorate in theology and was seeking a teaching position. One of his mentors at Wycliffe College, Prof. Oliver O'Donovan, had kindly written on his behalf to a number of institutions in the United Kingdom, among which was Regent's Park College, a Baptist school in the University of Oxford. He had also had an interview with the Catholic historian Michael M. Sheehan at St. Michael's College for a post-doctoral fellowship at the Pontifical Institute of Mediaeval Studies. And in this mix of quite different possibilities for his future was a two-hour interview at Central Baptist Seminary on Thursday, January 7, 1982. The school was then housed in a three-storey building at the end of Jonesville Crescent in Toronto, a short street that ran at a jaunty angle south of Eglinton Avenue.

Haykin had been invited to this interview with the academic dean of Central Baptist Seminary, Ted Barton, and the chairman of the board, Jack Hannah, to see if he might be a good fit for the faculty. Little did he know that his life for much of the next four decades would be bound up with this theological school. He had heard in December of 1981 of the death of Jack Scott, the chancellor of Central, and had asked Bruce Woods, his pastor at Stanley Avenue Baptist Church in Hamilton, if he thought there might be an opening at Central. He, in turn, had contacted Ted Barton and arranged for the interview. Haykin had no idea that Jack Scott, whom he remembered hearing once at a Stanley Avenue men's retreat at the Guelph Bible Conference Centre, was not a fulltime teacher at the school. And thus, his death did not automatically result in an opening at the school. Yet, this tiny link with Jack Scott connected Haykin to the very origins of the school in the early months of 1949, for Scott was the founding president of Central Baptist Seminary.

Founding a new school

When Jack Scott thought about the early days of this school, the idea that came most readily to his mind were the words of Jesus about his cousin, John the Baptist: he was "a burning and a shining light" (John 5:35, KJV). So was Central, Scott said in December of 1950: "God has ignited in Central Baptist Seminary a burning and shining light." What this meant, he went on to explain, was "a consuming passion" among the students "to make Christ known to every creature in this generation. The whole Seminary breathes this atmosphere. It is the constant concern of our united prayer life."[1] Evangelism, Christ-centredness, united prayer—these motifs also bring to mind the opening scenes of the Book of Acts and the apostolic revival at Pentecost

---

1   *Bulletin of Central Baptist Seminary* 1, no.1 (December 1950): 1.

CHAPTER ONE

Jack Scott

recorded there.

And yet, the ancient church's experience of Pentecost was not without controversy. Similarly, the founding of Central Baptist Seminary had not been free from serious contention. The immediate cause of the school's emergence was a split within the faculty and students of Toronto Baptist Seminary. This seminary, then, as now, was located next door to Jarvis Street Baptist Church, where the pastor at the time was the formidable T. T. Shields.

Shields had played an indispensable role in fighting liberal theology in the theology faculty at McMaster University in the 1920s, part of a larger struggle that historians now call the Fundamentalist-Modernist controversy, which engulfed religious denominations throughout

CHAPTER ONE

the North American continent.² At the height of this controversy in Ontario, Shields had founded Toronto Baptist Seminary and become its first president. Shields had also gone on to lead a body of churches based in Ontario and Quebec known as the Union of Regular Baptist Churches. His leadership throughout the 1930s and 1940s, however, had been fraught with one controversy after another. Finally in 1948 and 1949 there came the straw that broke the back of the proverbial camel: Shields removed the Dean of Toronto Baptist Seminary, W. Gordon Brown, from his position and Brown along with Jack Scott and other key Baptist leaders in Ontario—those in the body of churches known as the Union of Regular Baptist Churches—made the difficult but necessary decision to form a new school.

Brown had begun his full-time teaching career at Toronto Baptist Seminary in the fall of 1931. The influence of Shields upon Brown, by the latter's own admission, was enormous.³ Brown served faithfully both as a teacher and dean at Toronto Baptist Seminary until the division between him and Shields in 1948. Personality and temperament undoubtedly played major roles in this conflict between Shields and Brown, but at the heart of the split was also a vital difference of perspective about the nature of the seminary. Shields was averse to allowing students from another association of Baptist churches,

---

2   For the life and ministry of T. T. Shields, see especially Leslie K. Tarr, *Shields of Canada: T. T. Shields (1873-1955)* (Grand Rapids, MI: Baker Book House, 1967); idem, "Another Perspective on T. T. Shields and Fundamentalism" in *Baptists in Canada: Search for Identity Amidst Diversity*, ed. Jarold K. Zeman (Burlington, ON: G.R. Welch Co., Ltd., 1980), pp. 209-224; Arnold Dallimore, "T. T. Shields," *Reformation Today* 86 (July-August 1985): pp. 7-10; G. A. Rawlyk, "A. L. McCrimmon, H. P. Whidden, T. T. Shields, Christian Education, and McMaster University" in *Canadian Baptists and Christian Higher Education*, ed. G. A. Rawlyk (Kingston, ON; Montreal, QC: McGill-Queen's University Press, 1988), pp. 31-62; Doug A. Adams, "The War of the Worlds: The Militant Fundamentalism of Dr. Thomas Todhunter Shields and the Paradox of Modernity" (PhD thesis, The University of Western Ontario, 2015).

3   See Kenneth E. Hall, "Dr. W. Gordon Brown: a biography" (Unpublished essay, prepared as a paper for Church History III, taught by Charles Tipp, 1965), p. 32. This essay is housed in the Archives of Heritage College and Seminary, Cambridge, ON. The details regarding Brown in the rest of this paragraph are also taken from this source.

namely, the Fellowship of Independent Baptist Churches, into Toronto Baptist Seminary, while Brown "deliberately cultivated" links with the Fellowship and her ministers, and wanted their students in the school.[4]

A majority of the teachers and around 50 of the 75 students at the Seminary sided with Brown and formed, in January 1949, what would become Central Baptist Seminary.[5] Brown was the new school's first dean, a position he held till 1973, and Jack Scott, as noted, was the first president. At the time, Scott was also the pastor of Forward Baptist Church in Toronto.[6]

W. Gordon Brown

Without a doubt, Brown was the prime figure shaping Central Baptist Seminary for the first twenty-five years or so of its existence. He was born in 1904 in the village of Brownsville, near Tillsonburg in southern Ontario, a village that was named after his great-grandfather Brinton Paine Brown (1797-1883). Brinton Brown was the son of a Captain Benajah Brown (d.1805), who was a United Empire Loyalist.[7] In 1830 Brinton Brown was ordained as a New Connexion Methodist minister and eleven years later he moved to what is now Brownsville and soon organized a Methodist church in the village.[8] A

---

4   Hall, "Dr. W. Gordon Brown," pp. 37-38. See also the superb analysis of this split by Paul R. Wilson, "Torn Asunder: T. T. Shields, W. Gordon Brown, and the Schisms at Toronto Baptist Seminary and Within the Union of Regular Baptist Churches of Ontario and Quebec, 1948-1949," *McMaster Journal of Theology and Ministry* 19 (2017-2018): pp. 34-80.

5   The school was initially called the Canadian Baptist Seminary.

6   For the life of Scott, see Arnold Dallimore, *Only One Life: The Story of Dr. Jack Scott* (Hamilton, ON: Image Publishing, 1984). For his ministry at Forward Baptist Church, see Michael A. G. Haykin, Baiyu Andrew Song, and Paul Andrew Grey Gillespie, *"Behold, the Lamb of God": A centennial history of Forward Baptist Church, Toronto, 1919-2019* (Toronto, ON: Forward Baptist Church, 2019), pp. 56–79.

7   For a brief life of Brinton Paine Brown, see Anonymous, *Short Sketch of the Life of Brinton Paine Brown of Brownsville—Ontario* (Tillsonburg, ON: Liberal Book Press, 1904).

8   Pace "Dr. W. Gordon Brown: a biography" in *The History of Central Baptist Seminary*, ed. Gary W.

CHAPTER ONE

W. Gordon Brown

Baptist congregation was planted in the village in 1880 and Brinton Paine Brown's grandson, William James Hay Brown (1875–1935), briefly served as its minister in the first decade of the twentieth century.[9]

W. Gordon Brown was baptized by his father in 1913, a few years after his conversion. Following his studies at Humberside Collegiate

---

McHale (Gormley, ON: Central Baptist Seminary, 1993), [p. 9], who identifies Brinton Brown as "a Baptist pastor."

9   For a brief life of W. J. H. Brown, see [W. Gordon Brown,] *"To Testify ... the Grace of God": In Memoriam W.J.H. Brown* [(Toronto, ON: Toronto Baptist Seminary, 1935)].

CHAPTER ONE

Institute in Toronto, Brown won a scholarship to attend McMaster University. It was there that he encountered what he was then calling theological "modernism," that is, liberal theology, in the person of L. H. Marshall, the professor of homiletics. Marshall's appointment in the fall of 1925 initiated a three-year controversy in which Brown played a key role, supplying T. T. Shields with evidence of Marshall's erroneous views and also publishing a small newspaper that Brown called *The Prophet*, which was intensely critical of Marshall and the administration of McMaster University for supporting the modernist professor.

After graduating from McMaster University with his B.A. in 1925, Brown briefly served as the pastor of a Baptist cause in Orangeville. From 1927 to 1930, he also served as a part-time teacher at Toronto Baptist Seminary. It was in the fall of 1931 that he began teaching Greek, Hebrew, and the New Testament as a full-time professor at Toronto Baptist Seminary. It was during this period that he began to develop his course, "The Life of Christ," which became one of his major contributions to the academic formation of students over the years at Central Baptist Seminary. In 1930 he had had a term of study at The Southern Baptist Theological Seminary, where he took courses in Greek from the renowned New Testament scholar A. T. Robertson. Brown later used Robertson's *A Harmony of the Gospels* (1922) as the central textbook in this course on Christ's life.

Though Brown was teaching full-time at Toronto Baptist Seminary, he was also hard at work on his M.A. at the University of Toronto, which he received in 1935. He went on to fulfill all of the course requirements for a Ph.D. at Toronto and had written most of his thesis, but busyness during the 1930s, especially at Toronto Baptist Seminary, prevented him from finishing his doctorate. But Brown was a life-time student. For example, he went on to get a B.D.

CHAPTER ONE

from Winona Lake School of Theology in 1961.

"This seminary exists for the purposes of education"
The stories about Brown as a teacher are legion and many of them convey his no-nonsense approach to teaching and study. For many students from the 1950s to the early 1970s, their initial impressions of Brown were similar to the following remarks of Jack Hannah, who studied at Central in the 1960s and later served as the school's president in the late 1980s:

> I was introduced to Dean Brown in 1963 … I quickly concluded like most people in the assessment of the man that he was a brilliant scholar and an excellent teacher/communicator but was cold, distant, impersonal, detached and uncaring. I would soon learn that my assessment was wrong except for the teaching, scholar, and communication part.[10]

In the classroom, Brown was "austere, authoritative, and unbending."[11] He had an "icebergian finesse," in the words of Ted Angrove, who graduated in 1973.[12] Male students were always addressed simply by their surname and female students as "Miss——." When he called upon students to answer a question he had posed, Hannah noted, "you [had] better know the answer," or you would be told to "sit down, burn some midnight oil, and use some elbow grease before you come to class!" One of the benefits, Hannah later realized about

---

10 Jack Hannah, "Dr. W. Gordon Brown" (Handwritten 6-page ms., 2023, in the possession of Michael A. G. Haykin), [p. 1].
11 Hannah, "Dr. W. Gordon Brown," [p. 3].
12 Edward W. Angrove, "Memoires of a Dean By One of His Students" (Typed 3-page ms., January 9, 1997, in the possession of Michael A.G. Haykin), p. 2.

CHAPTER ONE

Jack Hannah

this approach, was that Brown was teaching his students to think on their feet.[13]

Brown's love of the academic world also came through in the classroom. At the opening chapel of the 1969–1970 academic year, Brown told the students:

> [T]his is an institution of learning. Those of you who have come here to get warm had better return to your churches—if they're warm enough! You have a minute to

---

13 Hannah, "Dr. W. Gordon Brown," [p. 3].

decide; please close the door quietly behind you.[14]

As Brown reiterated on another occasion: "This seminary exists for the purposes of education."[15] He would begin classes with a pithy prayer such as, "Let's pray. Dear Lord, give us more brains, more brains, Amen"![16] Richard Long, a student at Central in the 1970s, noted that Brown taught his "Life of Christ" course out of the Greek text and "he assumed you could follow along with his thinking about the nuances of the original language."[17] Brown's skill in handling the original languages of the Scriptures is evident also in the fact that he was one of a few scholars residing in Canada to be selected for the translation committee for the New International Version (NIV), which began its work in the late 1960s.[18] When Central Baptist Seminary was formed, Brown was also serving as pastor of Runnymede Baptist Church. This gave his teaching a strong pastoral aspect, but as time went on, it would entail significant stress as Brown sought to serve faithfully both the seminary and the church.[19] His administrative load at the seminary and his pastoral duties at the church also curtailed further contributions that Brown could have made in terms

---

14 Angrove, "Memoires of a Dean," p. 2.

15 Angrove, "Memoires of a Dean," p. 3.

16 Jack Hannah, "W. G. Brown: The Shape of His Life and Ministry (Interview Notes with Michael Haykin)" (5-page typescript ms., February 6, 2001), [p. 5].

17 Richard Long, Email to Michael A.G. Haykin, January 21, 2023.

18 For the list of all of the scholars involved in the production of the NIV, see "The NIV Committee on Bible Translation" (https://www.bible-researcher.com/niv-translators.html; accessed October 15, 2023). Three of the other scholars in Canada were Richard N. Longenecker and R. K. Harrison, both of whom were teaching at Wycliffe College, Toronto, and Bruce K. Waltke, then teaching at Regent College in Vancouver. According to Edith McCredie, Brown worked on translating the Gospel of John (Michael A.G. Haykin, "Interview with Edith McCredie, April 16, 1996" [5-page handwritten ms., in the possession of Michael A.G. Haykin], p. 4).

19 On Brown's pastorate at Runnymede, see [Chris Richardson and Rebekah Bedard Arthurs,] *Runnymede Community Church: Celebrating 100 Years. A Testament to God's Faithfulness and Grace 1911-2011* (Toronto: Runnymede Community Church, 2011), pp. 30–40.

of academic writing.

Richard Long has described Brown as "a master of time,"[20] that is, an expert in emphasizing, by personal example, the wise use of time and the importance of brevity. His sermons in the seminary chapel, as elsewhere, were marked by brevity, for instance, though they were always jam-packed with rich content. They were usually no more than 20 to 25 minutes. His passion for brevity was evident on one occasion when he was scheduled to speak after a number of other addresses—possibly at an ordination or conference. The other speakers on this occasion took far more time than they were allotted. So, Brown rose and simply quoted John 10:8, "All those who came before me were thieves and robbers" and then sat down again![21]

"Moments of meditation"[22]
W. Gordon Brown – February 20, 1972

"Jesus Christ came into the world to save sinners" [1 Timothy 1:15]. The story is in four Gospels, like the four points of a compass.

Matthew points east, for he was a Jew, once a hated tax-collector, whom Jesus turned into an apostle, a missionary to his own people. He put his message into a book to prove to his own people that Jesus was the Christ.

Mark points west. He helped his mother entertain Jesus and the Twelve. For a time, he worked with Paul and

---

20   Long, Email to Haykin, January 21, 2023.
21   Long, Email to Haykin, January 21, 2023.
22   For many years, Brown gave these extremely pithy "Moments of Meditation" on CFRB every Sunday morning. This particular one aired on Sunday morning, February 20, 1972.

> Barnabas, but later attached himself to Peter and heard him tell again and again the deeds of Jesus. Peter even called him his son. He put into a book the Gospel of Peter, apparently for the Romans.
>
> For the northern part of our compass take Dr. Luke, who worked with Paul in Europe, later accompanied him to Rome; stayed till Paul was executed. Paul became Luke's human inspiration and wrote what even a skeptic called the most beautiful book in the world.
>
> Our compass needs a south point, south to Egypt and its millions and across the teeming Mediterranean with a message for the whole world. That is John's, the last of the four Gospels, intended for all men everywhere, for he it is who says: The eternal Mind of God became man, and put up His tent among us, so that we could see His character, full of grace and truth [see John 1:14]. Jesus Christ ... there is no other way.

Yet, there was another side to Dean Brown that was evident in his keeping track of students after they had graduated, praying for both them and their children by name (Dr. Brown and his wife Louise—who was adept in Latin, Greek, and Hebrew and taught Greek at the seminary—never had any children of their own). He also invested himself in the lives of a number of international students. For example, when John Thomas came from India to study at the seminary in the 1960s, Dr. Brown frequently paid for his food, clothing, and accommodation out of his own pocket.[23] Thomas went back to India

---

23 Hannah, "Dr. W. Gordon Brown," [p. 5]. According to 1951 graduate Harold F. Banton, Brown was "really very tender hearted and compassionate ... If someone had a personal problem shared with

CHAPTER ONE

John Thomas

The installation of John Thomas as principal of Calcutta Bible College

CHAPTER ONE

to teach at the Calcutta Bible College, where he served as principal from 1984 to 1995. Brown's care for Thomas was repeated with a number of other students. Little wonder that many of them reckoned that Brown had an ongoing impact on their lives long after they had graduated.[24]

"Terrific grounding"
Ruth Oltmann

I have very fond memories of Dr. Brown. He was a wonderful man who encouraged me, a very young student who had a lot of problems to overcome. …

My time at central Baptist Seminary (1955–1959) solidified my faith and saw me through some very difficult times in the years after. It was terrific grounding in the Faith with solid facts. Although I never went into full-time Christian work per se, the fact I graduated from seminary helped me get … [a] job as I needed post-secondary education, and my job has opened some astounding doors of witness.

Dr. J. F. Holliday … and Dean Brown were the stalwarts of seminary during my time there. I never knew of any friction amongst the staff of the seminary in my days as a student. I think Dean Brown collected some very wise and competent men as teachers.

---

the Dean, it became top priority to try and find an acceptable solution." ("W. Gordon Brown, M.A., D.D." [3-page typescript ms., n.d., in the possession of Michael A.G. Haykin], p. 3).

24 See, for example, Hannah, "Dr. W. Gordon Brown," [p. 6].

CHAPTER ONE

The St. George campus

The seminary's first permanent locale was near the University of Toronto campus, at 225 St. George Street. This former home was purchased in 1949 for $35,000 with a downpayment of $17,500. Nine years later, extensive renovations led to, among other things, the construction of a new library and a new chapel. By the late 1950s, though, it was becoming evident that the building would be far too small if the number of students continued to increase. In 1955–1956, the student body reached a new high of 54.[25]

Among the teachers at the school during the early 1950s was a young theologian, Samuel J. Mikolaski, who celebrated his 100th birthday this year (2023). Mikolaski was a brilliant student who earned three degrees at the University of Western Ontario and then went on to obtain a D.Phil. from the University of Oxford. His academic interests were broad and included philosophy, political science, church history, and biblical studies. He taught ethics, philosophy, and Bible doctrine at Central in those early days. His later academic career included teaching at New Orleans Baptist Theological Seminary, North American Baptist Seminary, the presidency of Crandall University (then Atlantic Baptist College), Carey Hall, and Golden Gate Baptist Theological Seminary.[26] His tenure at Central was all-too brief.

Other teachers during the 1950s included: W. W. Fleischer, who taught Church History; Maurice Boillat, the French tutor (Central continued a tradition that had begun at Toronto Baptist Seminary, of including French in the curriculum with the hope that some of

---

[25] "Largest Freshmen Class Registers for New Term," *Bulletin of Central Baptist Seminary* 5, no.1 (October 1955), p. 1.

[26] "Former President Celebrates 100th Birthday" (https://www.crandallu.ca/2023/01/09/former-president-celebrates-100th-birthday/; accessed September 24, 2023).

CHAPTER ONE

225 George Street in downtown Toronto

The graduating class of 1953

the students would go on to serve in Quebec); Morley Hall, J. F. Holliday, B. Jeffrey, and J. C. Stern—these four pastors taught the four courses in Systematic Theology; and Dean Brown's wife, Louise, who taught English as well as first-year Greek and first-year Hebrew. One key addition to the teaching faculty came in 1959 when W. S. Whitcombe, a long-time friend of Brown's, was appointed to teach all of the Systematic Theology courses.[27] Also essential to the life of the school were the staff, some of whom were volunteers. Among them was Edith McCredie, who had an L.Th. from Toronto Baptist Seminary and who served faithfully as the full-time faculty secretary till June of 1974.[28]

"Edith McCredie, far more than a secretary"

When Central Baptist Seminary opened its doors at Forward Baptist Church in 1949, Edith McCredie was the secretary of Dean Brown. "Secretary," though, does not adequately describe Edith's contribution to the school. In one publication, she was described as a "business manager as well as bookkeeper, registrar as well as secretary, student counsellor as well as record keeper."

Edith McCredie

---

27 Johan D. Tangelder, "The History of the Central Baptist Seminary" (Unpublished essay, n.d.; in the possession of Michael A. G. Haykin), pp. 6-8.
28 "Miss McCredie Retires," *Central Baptist Seminary Bulletin* (July 1974): [p. 2].

> and "if the Seminary were a kingdom, she would be the power behind the throne." In another article, she was called a "gold mine of information." In her position at the Seminary, Edith had the privilege of becoming acquainted with many of the Lord's servants, both teachers and students, many of whom were, or became, pastors and missionaries. And she made it a point to keep in touch with a goodly number of them by letter after they had graduated. The esteem in which she was held by all was evident at Seminary gatherings and Fellowship Conventions by the number of former students who sought her out in order to speak with her. In 1981, Edith was given the Alumnus of the Year Award by the Seminary.

One of the highlights of the academic year was the spring graduation. In the words of Terry Madison, who graduated with a B.Th. in 1963:

> Graduation is a wonderful time in the life of any student. The years of hard work and diligent study are now to be rewarded. The labour of Seminary is now over and the deadlines for a multitude of assignments is past. The course of study, which in the beginning seemed so long in duration, is suddenly over. It is the end of one era of life and the entrance into another.[29]

During the 1950s and 1960s, a number of the men invited to be

---

29   Terry Madison, "Seminary Graduation 1963," *The Evangelical Baptist* 10, no. 8 (June 1963): p. 12.

CHAPTER ONE

the guest speakers at the graduations of the school reads like a who's who of the evangelical world in North America at that time: J. Sidlow Baxter, W.A. Criswell, and Robert G. Lee. A sizeable number of the graduates (way out of proportion to the size of the student body) during these years went on to have significant ministries in North America and overseas. To name but a few of these students from the first two decades of the school's existence—Frank and Marion Pickering, Bob Holmes, Paul Holliday, Lloyd Carr, George Bell, Maurice Boillat, Elisée Beau, Richard Holliday, John Bonham, Lester Laird, Don Whiteside, Roy Comrie, Linda Cannell, and D. A. Carson.

Gwyn and Roy Comrie

CHAPTER ONE

The staff and faculty in 1963

The graduating class of 1963. Marina Coldwell, who served for many years at both Central and Heritage as a faculty secretary and who kept extensive records of the life of the school for all of the decades of her service, is in the very middle of the second row

CHAPTER ONE

Marina Coldwell

A decade of significant changes

After two decades of carrying the chief administrative load of the seminary, full-time teaching at the school, as well as being the senior pastor at Runnymede Baptist Church and teaching at Richmond College, a liberal arts school in Toronto that had been founded in 1967, it is no surprise that the strain and stress of all of this administration and teaching took their toll on Dean Brown. In the fall of 1971, Brown had what would then have been termed a "nervous breakdown."[30] The Board of Directors released a statement on November 23 stating that it was convinced Brown had been under "severe tension"

---

30 According to E. Sidney Kerr, who was the president of Central from 1960–1963, Kerr advised Brown to either resign from Runnymede's pastorate or quit the deanship at Central. Brown didn't listen to him and the result, according to Kerr, was Brown's "nervous breakdown." (Michael Haykin, "Interview with Sid Kerr, July 7, 1996" [Transcript in the personal possession of Michael Haykin]).

CHAPTER ONE

for a while. They were thus relieving him of all of his "seminary responsibilities" till May 31, 1972. This decision was only taken after "long and careful consideration and prayer."[31] Jack Hannah, who was present in his capacity as the president of the Alumni Association, remembers very clearly the board members actually weeping as they unanimously voted in favour of this decision.[32] Their love for Brown was quite evident.

The Board appointed Denzil Raymer (1915–1978) as interim dean. Raymer had been teaching in a full-time capacity at Central since 1966. When it became obvious that Brown was not going to be able to resume his duties as dean in the summer of 1972, Raymer was appointed as the dean at their September board meeting.[33] That year he also earned his M.A. in Old Testament from Wheaton College.[34] He would lead the school as dean till his untimely death six years later.

The dawn of 1972 also witnessed a move of the school from St. George Street in downtown Toronto to North York in the northeast part of Metro Toronto. The growth of the student body—there were over forty incoming students in the fall of 1972—necessitated the move to a larger facility. A modern three-story building was built for the school at 95 Jonesville Crescent, near the intersection of Eglinton Avenue and Victoria Park Avenue. The school commenced classes in this new locale in the first week of January 1973, and a few weeks later, at the official open house, more than 700 came to celebrate the move to the new locale. Initially, the school was located on the first

---

31 W. H. MacBain, Chairman of the Board of Directors, Letter to Fellowship Baptist Pastors, November 23, 1971 (Archives of Heritage College and Seminary).
32 Hannah, "W. G. Brown: The Shape of His Life and Ministry," [p. 3].
33 "Other Faculty Changes," *Central Baptist Seminary Bulletin* (October 1972): [p. 1].
34 For an overview of his life and ministry, see "Dean Denzill Edwin Raymer" in *History of Central Baptist Seminary*, ed. McHale, [pp. 83–87].

CHAPTER ONE

Denzill Raymer

and third floors and the second floor was rented. In the 1980s, however, the school would take over the second floor, renovating a large portion of it for the school's chapel, which would be named the Dr. Jack Scott Memorial Chapel.[35]

In 1973, when the school celebrated its twenty-fifth anniversary, the school had graduated over 400 students. In its first official publication in 1973—the January issue of the *Central Baptist Seminary Bulletin*—it was stated that this achievement was owing totally to the Lord's faithfulness, an explicit allusion to the school's hymn, Thomas Chisholm's (1866–1960) "Great is Thy Faithfulness," based on Lamentations 3:23.[36] The graduation speaker that year was Arnold

---

35 "Chapel Furnishings," *Just Between Friends* 1, no. 3 (Spring 1984): [pp. 8–9].
36 "25th Graduation on May 1st," *Central Baptist Seminary Bulletin* (January 1973): [p. 1].

CHAPTER ONE

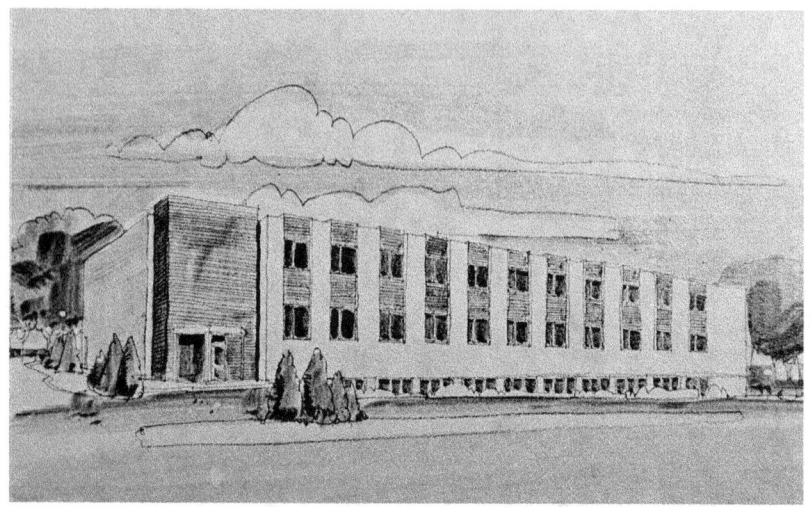

Central Baptist Seminary, according to an artist's conception prior to its being built

Dallimore (1911–1998), the pastor of the Fellowship Baptist in Cottam and the author of the first volume of a then-projected two-volume work on the life of the Anglican evangelist George Whitefield (1714–1770). Dallimore's two-volume biography of Whitefield, now published by the Banner of Truth, was to have an enormous worldwide impact for good.[37]

1973 and 1974 saw a number of significant changes in the life of the school. In 1973, Richard Mitchell, who had taught part-time at Central in the 1960s while pastoring at High Park Baptist Church in Toronto, was appointed to the full-time faculty as professor of New

---

[37] For a study of Dallimore's life and work, see especially Ian Hugh Clary, *Reformed Evangelicalism and the Search for a Usable Past: The Historiography of Arnold Dallimore, Pastor-Historian*, Reformed Historical Theology, vol.61 (Göttingen: Vandenhoeck & Ruprecht, 2020). For a brief synopsis of his life and work, see also Michael A. G. Haykin, "Dr. Arnold Dallimore" in *Fellowship Baptist Trailblazers: Life Stories of Pastors and Missionaries*, comp. Fred A. Vaughan (Belleville, ON: Guardian Books, 2002), 2:73–78; *idem*, "Remembering Arnold Dallimore and His Books," *The Banner of Truth* (August-September 2022), pp. 707–708

CHAPTER ONE

Richard Mitchell

Testament. He taught diligently till Central's merger with London in 1993. Stanley K. Fowler, who was to play a critical role in the life of Central and Heritage, later commented about Mitchell's service: "There are not many professors who can teach with as much versatility as Richard, and not many with enough of a servant's heart to stick with it through the good times and the bad times."[38]

The following year, Donald Loveday, the president of the school, stepped down to become the Dean of Students and the school administrator, while Jack Scott, the first president of the school, was elected to succeed Loveday. A new librarian was appointed in the

---

38 Stanley K. Fowler, "A Tribute to Richard Mitchell" in *History of Central Baptist Seminary*, ed. McHale, [pp. 95–96].

person of Ruth Kraulis (1917–2005). Kraulis was a native of Latvia and had earned her Magister of Philology in Classics at the University of Latvia in the midst of World War II. She fled Latvia for Sweden during the latter days of the war and emigrated with her family to Toronto in 1948. She earned bachelor and master degrees in library science and came to Central from North York Public Library, where she had been the Head of Technical Services for 13 years. She served faithfully at Central from 1974 to 1983.

During this decade, a number of courses were taught by part-time instructors. For example, Ken Davis, who was on the faculty of the University of Waterloo and would become one of North America's leading experts on sixteenth-century Anabaptism, taught church history. And in 1975, Douglas Shantz, who would also have a distinguished academic career at the University of Calgary as an expert in German Pietism, was appointed to teach Systematic Theology. In the fall of 1977, the full-time faculty were strengthened further with the addition of Emily Turansky as Dean of Women and Professor of Christian Education and Paul T. Holliday as Professor of Theology.

These years also saw a significant surge in student enrollment. In the academic year 1970–1971, there were 75 students taking a variety of programs at the seminary. Eight years later, in 1977–1978, that number stood at 134. With the second highest enrolment of students in the history of the school (the highest was during 1975–1976, when there were 135 registered for courses at the school), the future seemed rosy indeed. But there were major challenges just around the corner.

CHAPTER ONE

"An earthiness and real hands-on feel"
Mark Woods

Mark Woods

I entered Central Baptist Seminary in the second year of my M.Div. degree studies after taking my first year at a non-denominational seminary in Columbia, South Carolina. Immediately I was struck by the feeling that my seminary world view had shrunk dramatically. In Columbia I was exposed to world-class scholars and a much wider horizon of non-Baptistic perspectives than at Central. At first, this seemed like a negative thing, but as time went on, I began to appreciate the closeness and family feel that CBS presented. Most of our professors were, or had been Fellowship Baptist pastors, and we had a steady stream of active pastors speaking in our chapel services. This served to focus my attention more intently on the practical aspects of church life and pastoral work. It was refreshing to hear men speak of their preaching styles, outreach initiatives, pastoral counselling and church business experiences, rather than just reading of these things from a text book, or hearing a national "expert" expound on them in front of a thousand students in chapel. In a word, there was an

> earthiness and real hands-on feel to the instruction I was receiving. This served me well in terms of preparation to do ministry with real people in real churches with real day-to-day issues and also gave me a confidence that as an everyday person with foibles just the same as anyone else, I could enter pastoral work as a humble servant of God, allowing His Spirit to work through me in all my endeavours.

Facing setbacks

Between the fall of 1978 and that of 1979, there occurred the deaths of Denzill Raymer, the dean of the school, W. Gordon Brown, dean emeritus, and Paul Holliday, who had succeeded Jack Scott as president in January of 1979 and was thus in office less than a year. Two years later, on December 8, 1981, Jack Scott, who had become the chancellor of Central at the beginning of 1979, also passed away. Filling the shoes of these men was no easy task. But by 1980, the school had found a new academic dean in the person of Ted Barton, who had been appointed the professor of biblical studies and biblical languages two years earlier. Barton was a two-time graduate of Central and had also earned an M.A. at the University of Toronto in 1965. When he was appointed dean, he was enrolled in a DMin programme at Trinity Evangelical Divinity School in Illinois. Over the next number of years, he played a critical role in the life of Central. His teaching was energetic and impactful. Ruth Cosman Edwards remembers watching "with enthusiasm when Mr. Barton would pace back and forth with such excitement many of us were afraid he'd fall

CHAPTER ONE

Ted and Margaret Barton

off the chapel platform."³⁹ He left the office of dean in 1985.⁴⁰

> ### "One of the greatest experiences of my life"
> #### Phillip Holliday
>
> My time at CBS was one of the greatest experiences of my life. Three years before I came to Central, while studying at the University of Windsor, I was involved in a terrible accident in which someone died. Then two years before I came my father, Paul Holliday, died of cancer at the age of 49. So, first of all, my first year at Central was a time of great spiritual and emotional healing for me. The students

---

39 Ruth Cosman Edwards, Email to Michael Haykin, September 13, 2023.
40 See "Dr. G.E. (Ted) Barton" in *History of Central Baptist Seminary*, ed. McHale, [pp. 71–72]. For the notice of his retirement, see "In Honor and Appreciation," *Just between Friends* 2, no. 3 (Summer 1985): [p. 5].

CHAPTER ONE

and the faculty were loving and supportive in many ways.

I ran out of money after my first year so I took a job as a night court clerk at the Old City Hall provincial court house and studied at Central part-time. I really enjoyed being able to take fewer courses at the time, as I found that I could enjoy, absorb, and appreciate them all the more. I was also able to serve as the Assistant Pastor at Christie St. Baptist Church.

Phillip Holliday

I was able to grow in my love for God, his word, and others in so many ways at Central. Moreover, as I look back at those years at Central, one of the things that I really valued was that the school environment allowed for differences of opinion in theology and biblical interpretation, among both the faculty and students. I believe this helped us to think more deeply and be stronger in our faith.

CHAPTER ONE

"A spiritual and intellectual awakening"
Scott Dyer

Scott Dyer

I attended Central Baptist Seminary from 1980 to 1984 in what turned out to be a seminal turning point of my life. Shortly before attending the seminary, I had been living a very rebellious lifestyle that was fueled by drug and alcohol abuse and that masked an inner angst that I barely understood at the time. I was attending Campbell Baptist Church in Windsor, Ontario, and in the summer of 1979 I came in contact with a student youth leader from Central who had a tremendous impact on my life and eventually convinced me to attend the seminary.

Attending Central gave rise to both a spiritual and intellectual awakening. Whole new vistas of knowledge and wisdom were opened up to me through the excellent professors and the materials I was exposed to. It was truly a life-transforming experience. Even though I did not end up in professional ministry, the skills I developed have been put to good use through over forty years of teaching

> in the local church, writing, and now even podcasting. I look back with great fondness and gratitude for the years I spend at Central and the lifelong friends and dialogue partners I met there.

Filling the office of interim president at this time was Dr. James G. Wetherall, the pastor of High Park Baptist Church in Toronto. Wetherall was also a two-time Central graduate and had gone on to receive his doctorate from the University of Basel in 1977. Since he continued in the role of pastor at High Park, much of the leadership for the day-to-day life of the school fell into the lap of Barton. Wetherall's presidency concluded two years later, in the summer of 1982, and Central was again without a president.

Dr. Hal MacBain served on an interim basis as the president for the academic year 1982–1983. Then, in the summer of 1983, George Bell accepted a call to be Central's eighth president. A graduate of Central (BTh, 1954), Bell had pastored Baptist churches in Montreal, Winnipeg, and Toronto. For the ten years prior to his call to Central's presidency, Bell had served as the director of the Ontario region of the Fellowship of Evangelical Baptist Churches in Canada. Embracing the leadership of Central, he was very conscious that in "God's providence" Central had "suffered setbacks and changes in leadership." This had meant that Central's constituency, upon whom the school relied for students and income, increasingly had no first-hand knowledge of what was going on at the school.[41] Bell was determined to reverse this trend and to that end had initiated what he called "Renovation '83." This project entailed a total renovation of the second floor of the

---

41 George D. Bell, Letter to Friend[s] of C.B.S., April, 1984. For a biographical sketch of Bell and his wife Gwen, see "Dr. George Bell" in *History of Central Baptist Seminary*, ed. McHale, [pp. 73–74].

CHAPTER ONE

James Wetherall

George and Gwen Bell

CHAPTER ONE

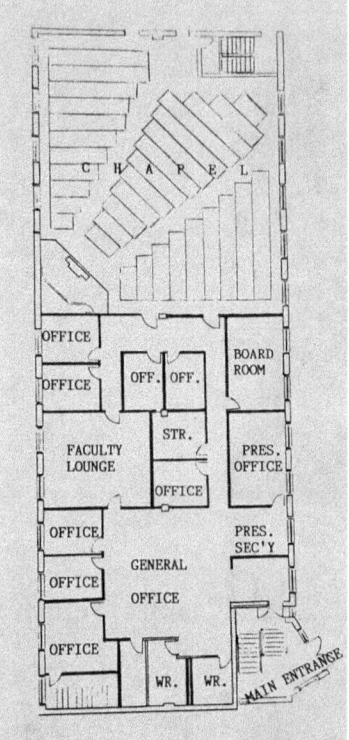

The projected renovation of the second floor of the seminary building

The Sounds of Praise

seminary building (including a chapel named after Jack Scott) with the expectation that God would bring a growing number of students to the school. George and his wife Gwen also spent a considerable amount of time travelling to churches on weekends to help raise the profile of the school and encourage support for Central. The singing group "The Sounds of Praise" (comprised of Meredith Hisey, Debbie DaSilva, and Brian Mullins) frequently travelled with them.

"The many times we sang 'Great is Thy Faithfulness' "
Sandy Ryerse

Sandy and Rick Ryerse

While most of my friends headed off to larger and better-known schools, God led me to Central Baptist Seminary, a modest-sized school in the big city of Toronto. I loved that the school was smaller. I loved that there were no dorms. I loved that there were students of all ages. But mostly, I loved that our professors taught and treated us like adults who planned on living our lives like godly men and women in whatever profession God was leading us to.

Beyond the many lifelong relationships I still hold dear from my days at Central, my greatest memory would have to be the many times we sang "Great is Thy Faithfulness" as a school family. The deep worship drew me ever deeper in my commitment to God.

"Our love for God's movement in history"
McTair Wall and Suzanne Lambert-Wall

McTair Wall and Suzanne Lambert-Wall

We now realize that CBS was probably the most formative experience in our spiritual and theological journey in developing a deep love for Scripture, for its careful interpretation and for communicating its truth cross-culturally. It was in this small community that our lives were

> enmeshed with those of professors and students who were passionate about God, his word, and his world. The approachability of professors had a lasting impact upon us. They reminded us that they were also disciples of Jesus—learners as we were. This openness modeled what we were hoped to be like in our future ministry. The basic orientation of our strong evangelical identity was also formed and hammered out at CBS. We learned about critical respectful engagement with Scripture and the world. This was informed by the depth of the evangelical heritage that runs throughout Church history. It was at CBS that our love for God's movement in history took shape. CBS taught us that if God has always used ordinary people to do extraordinary things, he can also use us to accomplish his purposes in our day.

"A quality faculty"[42]

In the fall of 1984, conscious of the need to attract high school students, Bell led the school to rebrand itself as "Central Baptist Seminary and Bible College."[43] He also knew that key to a school's flourishing were the faculty. Over the next four years, a significant number of new faces were added to the roster of full-time teachers and staff:

- Michael Haykin had been hired in the fall of 1982 to teach church history and Bible;

---

42 This is the description of the faculty in "Management Team," *Just between Friends* (Summer 1988): [p. 6].

43 "A New Name," *Just between Friends* 2, no. 1 (Fall 1984): [p. 4].

- John Greb, who had studied under W. Gordon Brown in the 1960s, was appointed administrator in 1984;[44]
- John Wilson—a gifted teacher who had taught at Grand Rapids Bible College since 1952 and had been interim dean at Central in 1979–1980 after the death of Denzill Raymer—became the academic dean in the summer of 1985 after Ted Barton stepped down from this role;[45]
- John W. Gunn, who had been pastoring at Freelton Baptist Church, was appointed in 1985 as registrar;[46]
- In the fall of 1986, Jim Rendle, an experienced church planter within the Fellowship of Evangelical Baptist Churches, joined the faculty;
- Don Clark, who had pastored Fellowship Baptist churches in Toronto and Lindsay, joined the full-time faculty in 1987;
- In the winter of 1987, Hugh Rendle became the new librarian;[47]
- Stanley K. Fowler, who had been teaching part-time at the seminary since 1980, came on as a full-time professor of theology in 1988;[48]
- And finally, in August of 1988, Terry Giles was appointed professor of Old Testament studies—Terry

---

44 "New Appointments," *Just between Friends* 1, no. 3 (Spring 1984): [p. 12].
45 *Just between Friends* 2, no. 3 (Summer 1985): [p. 3]. See also the biographical sketch in *History of Central Baptist Seminary*, ed. McHale, [p. 89].
46 See the notice of his being hired in *Just between Friends* 2, no. 4 (Fall 1985): [p. 3].
47 "Meet the New Librarian," *Just between Friends* (Winter 1987): [p. 4].
48 Richard Mitchell, "Rev. Stanley K. Fowler" in *History of Central Baptist Seminary*, ed. McHale, [pp. 76–77]. Se also the brief biography in "Faculty Focus," *Just between Friends* [Fall 1988]: [p. 5].

CHAPTER ONE

earned his PhD from Michigan State University the following February.[49]

Central faculty in 1988

John Wilson

49 "Introducing ...," *Just between Friends* (Summer 1988): [p. 1]; "Congratulations," *Just between Friends* [Winter 1989]: [p. 2].

CHAPTER ONE

This was indeed a quality faculty. Many of the students studying at the school during the tenure of these faculty members have remembered them with great fondness for the impact that they made on their lives. Tim Kerr, for example, has written:

> My memories of Central Baptist Seminary mostly involve certain professors who left a deep mark on me. I met my wife there—undoubtedly the greatest gift Central gave me. I remember Dr. Wilson's class on Romans that was life changing for me and imparted a deep love of Romans that remains to this day. I remember Mr. Mitchell's brutal Hermeneutics class which I didn't enjoy at the time, but have since come to realize was one of the most important classes I took during my 4 years in Seminary. I remember Dr. Stan Fowler, who was an incisive thinker and proceeded by conviction rather than popular opinions on a whole host of theological matters. I remember Dr. Michael Haykin introducing me to the great Puritan John Owen. I have been a huge fan ever since. He made church history come alive, and I owe my present love of the writings of Saint Augustine to him. Central taught me to love learning and reading. I'll be forever grateful.[50]

Tim's sister-in-law, Ruth Cosman Edwards, was in full agreement: "Seminary changed my life. … I've never for one moment since graduation ever regretted such privileged years to sit and learn at the feet of wonderful men and women of God."[51] Similarly, Alex Pacis, who has had a remarkable ministry of church planting, noted, "I can not

---

50 Tim Kerr, Email to Michael Haykin, September 14, 2023.
51 Edwards, Email to Haykin, September 13, 2023.

imagine being able to function in my position today without the formation time that I experienced at CBS. The relationship between us as students and the professors were basically an embarkation of reliving the life of Jesus, the apostles and early church leaders. Memorable times, special times, times well spent that set me for my whole lifetime."[52] And as Nicholas Miles also reflected more generally: "Certain teachers and moments generated lasting cherished memories that looking back provided deeper values than when first appreciated. … As the years went by, I often reminisced on what was learned from the examples of those days past. The key is these impressions and lessons lasted—they were things God was able to continually use and the value of that education was never lost."[53]

Of course, there were some of the students who were chaffing at the bit to get through school and out into full-time ministry. Dr. Hal McBain, who was serving as the chancellor during this period of time, wisely told them, "Prepare for the last ten years of your ministry."[54]

"Lord … Unite us"

In the midst of such blessing and behind the scenes, as it were, the school was having major financial problems. In March of 1988, the Board of Directors created a Management Team "to monitor areas such as relocation, recruitment and finances."[55] This body included Jack Hannah as its chairman as well as George Bell, John Greb, Roy W. Lawson—the general secretary of the Fellowship—and some

---

52 Alex Pacis, Email to Michael Haykin, September 21, 2023.
53 Nicholas Miles, Email to Michael Haykin, October 4, 2023.
54 Cited Richard Mitchell, "Seminary Information" (2-page ms., September 21, 2023, in the possession of Michael Haykin), [p. 1].
55 "Management Team." The minutes of the meetings of the Management Team from March 2, 1988, to March 29, 1989 are in the Archives of Heritage Seminary and College as a file entitled "Management Team."

local pastors and businessmen. During the course of 1988, there was a long discussion about relocating the seminary. Initially, there was significant enthusiasm about moving to Stouffville to be adjacent to Springvale Baptist Church. Such a move and putting up a new building, it was reckoned, would require around 6 million dollars.[56] At the April 5 meeting of this team, though, it was noted ominously, "Finances continue to haunt us."[57] At the conclusion of this meeting, a motion was made and passed to transfer ownership of the school to the Fellowship. Right from the outset of his presidency, George Bell had been rightly convinced that the "future of C.B.S. and of our Fellowship are closely intertwined."[58] But it became clear that the Fellowship did not wish to assume ownership of the school. And after numerous meetings with the leadership at Springvale, the plans to relocate there also came to nought.

By the summer of 1988, it was evident that donations were not at all matching expenses and that a move was needed. In October, it was suggested that the school pursue a "consortium with Redeemer College,"[59] now Redeemer University, which was located on a brand-new campus in Ancaster with 300 students or so.[60] This would have been a fabulous opportunity for Central, but it too failed to pan out.

In a detailed report brought to the Management Team during 1988, it was noted that there was an "insufficient donor base and commitment level among our churches toward CBS." In large part, it was suggested that this was due to the perception among potentially-supporting churches that the school lacked "financial responsibility"

---

56 Minutes for March 30, 1988 ("Management Team"), pp. 1–2.
57 Minutes for April 5, 1988 ("Management Team"), p. 1.
58 Bell, Letter to Friend[s] of C.B.S., April, 1984.
59 Minutes for October 11, 1988 ("Management Team"), p. 1.
60 "History of Redeemer University: First 10 Years" (https://libguides.redeemer.ca/c.php?g=730288&p=5248490; accessed October 29, 2023).

and "appropriate long term planning." Moreover, the report bluntly stated that the Board of Directors had failed "to recognize the kind of transitions that have been taking place within the Fellowship, the evangelical community, and the Canadian social fabric as a whole" so as to chart a course for the school to "establish itself as a strong theological institution."[61]

The following year, an offer of 2.7 million dollars for the school building was accepted. This offer allowed the school to continue at its Jonesville location till the summer of 1991.[62] This sale, however, did not essentially alleviate the ongoing crisis at the school. At a faculty meeting on August 31, 1989, the faculty were informed that none of their jobs were guaranteed beyond the following April. And a week later, on Thursday, September 7, the Board of Directors declared bankruptcy and voted to turn over all of the school's assets to the Fellowship of Evangelical Baptist Churches. The general secretary of the Fellowship, Roy Lawson, when informed of this decision, was at a loss for words.[63] That November, when the motion was raised to pursue the ownership of Central at the national convention of the Fellowship, the motion passed. Yet, there was considerable negativity expressed about the decision by some of the delegates.[64] As it turned out, this ownership never transpired.

By 1989, George Bell had stepped down as president. He was briefly replaced by Jack Hannah, who would later joke that his claim to fame was that he was the shortest-serving president of Central! Over the next couple of years, a number of the faculty whom Bell

---

61 "Management Team Report: Critical Factors in future Development of Central Baptist Seminary" ("Management Team"), [p. 2].
62 "Sold," *Just between Friends* [Spring 1989]: [p. 1].
63 Stan Fowler, Conversation with Michael Haykin, September 9, 1989, as recorded in Michael Haykin, "Notebook 5" (Personal diary, January 1, 1989–December 9, 1989), p. 120.
64 Michael Haykin, "Notebook 5A" (Personal diary, October 24, 1989–December 31, 1989), p. 8.

CHAPTER ONE

Stan Fowler

had assembled either left or were let go from the school. In February of 1991, Haykin felt that "the situation at Central [was] again grim."[65] A move to Willowdale Baptist Church, which was in the heart of North York and not far from Central's Jonesville locale, was considered. Also on the table was the possibility of a merger with London Baptist Bible College and Seminary and/or Toronto Baptist Seminary in downtown Toronto. Haykin was certain that any discussion with either of them was bound to fail. In fact, he was convinced that Central had no future.[66] Providentially, both judgments turned out to be quite wrong.

In the summer of 1991, the school relocated to Gormley and Stan Fowler was appointed acting president. This appointment turned out to be a real Godsend. Without Fowler's prudent and capable leadership between 1991 and 1993, Haykin's belief that there was no future

---

65 Michael Haykin, "Notebook 7" (Personal diary, December 19, 1990–November 4, 1991), p. 33.
66 Haykin, "Notebook 7," pp. 35–36.

for Central might well have come true. As it was, when a committee composed of men from London and from Central was set up in August of 1992 to investigate the possibility of a full merger between the two schools, Haykin prayed, "Lord, please bring this to pass! Unite us—not only institutionally—but in our hearts."[67]

"I encountered three realities"
Darryl Dash

When I enrolled at Central Baptist Seminary in 1988, I encountered three realities that shaped me and my ministry. The first was the quality of education. Professors like Stan Fowler and Michael Haykin helped me think Christianly and love the Lord. I sometimes wish I could go back and enjoy those classes again. The teaching and the input of the professors deeply influenced me and my ministry. The second was the student body. I made friendships then that have lasted 35 years. These friendships also helped to form me. Finally, the leaders of the seminary influenced me. I remember President George Bell challenging me about a character issue. I witnessed leaders wrestle with financial challenges that threatened the survival of the school. They showed me what it looks like to lead well when facing hardship. I can't overstate the importance of these years or the quality of Christian education I received. I'm grateful.

---

67 Michael Haykin, "Notebook 11" (Personal diary, August 21, 1992–December 28, 1992), p. 11.

"A life-changing experience"
Trevor Robotham

Trevor Robotham

CBS was a welcoming but also challenging environment in which one was forced to hammer out one's beliefs and practices. This was unique because of the relatively small student body who were often from different parts of the world with different experiences, practices and perspectives. This taught us to often agree to disagree, yet in the same way, when it came to the essentials, hold fast in love for our Lord Jesus and to respect one another. Also, because of the size of the student body, we were able to develop long and caring relationships with some of our instructors. For me, I found CBS to be a life-changing experience which I will forever be grateful for and cherish. I would like to thank all of the faculty at CBS for their part in helping to equip and prepare me for ministry.

2

"Truth aflame": A history of London Baptist Bible College and Seminary, 1976–1993

The desire for a new school in London

The city of London, Ontario, has been something of a Bible belt in Ontario with a history of bible colleges. In 1935, for instance, Dr. J. Wilmot Mahood started a school called London Bible Institute which was run out of London Gospel Tabernacle. The school was later named London College of Bible and Missions (LCBM). In 1968 LCBM merged with Toronto Bible College (TBC) to form Ontario Bible College and relocated to Spadina Avenue in Toronto. Over the next fifty years, this school, now known as Tyndale University, went through a variety of changes and is currently located on Bayview Avenue.[1] The merger between LCBM and TBC left a vacuum in the city of London, which in turn fueled a desire to see the founding

---

1 For this history, see Timothy Larsen and Jon Vickery, *For Christ in Canada: A History of Tyndale Seminary, 1976-2001* (Toronto, ON: Tyndale University College & Seminary, 2004), pp. 11–25.

CHAPTER TWO

The initial board of London Baptist Seminary

of a new school. In particular, five Baptist pastors and a missionary—Reuben Brubacher, Fred Howard, David Irwin, Reginald Snell, Robert Robinson, and missionary Melbourne Cuthbert—who were part of the Fellowship of Evangelical Baptist Churches (FEBC) were drawn together by an interest to start a new school.

The motivation behind starting a new school was then, in part, geographical. However, a second, and probably more important, reason was theological. The founding board wanted to offer an alternative to Central Baptist, since they believed a school with different theological convictions was needed. In particular, Central did not have an official theological stance on eschatology. Those who wanted a new school in London desired a firm commitment to premillennial dispensationalism. Such schools existed in the United States—such as Dallas Theological Seminary—and Canadians would go to the United States for school and not return. A new school in London would be able to offer a premillennial distinctive for those in the FEBC who could then remain in Canada for their theological studies. However, there was a third motivation as well, and this involved a growing dissatisfaction with the state of the FEBC. At the time, the head office of the FEBC was in Toronto and there was no Ontario region. A group wanted to start what was proposed as the Fellowship of Evangelical Baptists Churches Ontario Region (FEBCOR). The desire was to start a denominational region that had more independence and an ability to be self-governed. However, there were some FEBC leaders strongly against the idea of starting FEBCOR, and when it was brought to a vote at a FEBC gathering, the motion to start FEBCOR was defeated. Two of the men who wanted to make FEBCOR a reality were Robert Robinson and David Irwin. With the idea of FEBCOR defeated, they nevertheless still had a desire to see more churches planted and to have more autonomy from the Toronto leadership. Through a new school, they believed they could achieve such autonomy, and through its graduates they could see the planting of more independent Baptist Churches in Ontario. These three motivations behind the starting of a new school in London reveal the complex relationship that London had with the FEBC, not only at its inception, but throughout its seventeen-year history. When the decision had been formally made to start the school, Reuben Brubacher, one of the six founders, believed that his son, Marvin Brubacher, should be contacted.[2]

Marvin Brubacher was a graduate of Tennessee Temple University and in 1974 he was hired to work there as Residence Director and also to teach Greek. He received a letter about the plans to start the new school in London in the fall of 1975 and with it an invitation to be a member of the staff. Brubacher, however, also believed that another

---

2 Jonathan N. Cleland, "Interview with Gerry Benn, Liz Benn, and David Barker, London, Ontario, February 1, 2023"; *idem*, "Zoom interview with Marvin Brubacher, February 23, 2023."

person, Gerald D.A. Benn, should be involved in the school. Benn was a former teacher of Brubacher, a fellow Canadian, and a graduate of London College of Bible and Missions, making him a great fit for the London area. Although Benn was reluctant, Brubacher wanted him to pursue the call. In fact, Brubacher was so committed that he even wrote back to the board and mailed them Benn's résumé![3]

On October 27, 1975, both Brubacher and Benn traveled to Brantford to meet with the six men behind the plans for the new school. Whatever doubts Brubacher and Benn had ahead of this meeting, when the two of them left to fly back to the States, they both knew that this was what God was calling them to do. Once they got back to Tennessee, Brubacher and Benn met weekly to start mapping out plans for the school, while the board in London worked on student recruitment.[4]

London Baptist Seminary becomes a reality

The board started meeting monthly, right up to the start of the first school year. The board initially wanted to call the new venture the Canadian Baptist Bible College. However, the government refused to incorporate the school under this name. Next, "Baptist Bible College of Canada" was suggested.[5] This too was rejected. Eventually they chose the name London Baptist Seminary (LBS).[6] The initially-suggested nomenclature provides an important clue to the original vision for the school. The board saw LBS as serving a variety of

---

3   Cleland, "Zoom interview with Brubacher, February 23, 2023."
4   Cleland, "Interview with Benn, Benn, and Barker, February 1, 2023"; *idem*, "Zoom interview with Brubacher, February 23, 2023."
5   "Canadian Baptist Bible College Minutes of Board Meeting dated June 14, 1976," p. 2 (Canadian Baptist Bible College Minutes File, Box: LBBC/S Files B. Irwin Board of Governors Board Committees, Archives of Heritage College and Seminary).
6   "Canadian Baptist Bible College Board Meeting Minutes Monday, Aug. 23rd, 1976," p.1 (Canadian Baptist Bible College Minutes File).

conservative Baptists across Canada, whatever their denominational affiliation. The majority of the board, however, still saw themselves as a FEBC school.

Nevertheless, there was an ongoing tension between the school and the FEBC. At a board meeting on September 8, 1976, one day after the official opening, a discussion transpired about the school's relation to the FEBC. A part of this discussion revolved around whether or not to ask Dr. Jack Watt, the then-current secretary of FEBC, to come and speak at the chapel. It was brought to a vote, and although the motion carried by a majority,[7] it was obvious, for at least some on the board, that there was a tension with being connected with the FEBC. This tension existed for those observing the start of the new school as well. Although there was a cohort that was excited about the start of London, there were others in the FEBC who questioned why another school, in addition to Central Baptist Seminary, was needed. And for some, this questioning was expressed in a degree of hostility to the new school. W. Gordon Brown, Central Seminary's dean, for instance, mailed to Benn a letter expressing his strong disagreement with the opening of another school.[8]

The school began its first year on September 7, 1976, with 37 college students. The Convocation Service was held on September 24, with Dave Irwin, chairman of the board, giving the message, and Robert Robinson, the Vice Chairman, pronouncing the benediction.[9] In that first school year, Benn served as the president and Brubacher as the dean of students. Both Benn and Brubacher also served as faculty, with Benn teaching courses in Old Testament, New Testament,

---

7 "Canadian Baptist Bible College—Board Meeting Minutes, Wednesday, September 8, 1976," p.1 (Canadian Baptist Bible College Minutes File).
8 Cleland, "Interview with Benn, Benn, and Barker, February 1, 2023."
9 "Fall Convocation Service, September 24, 1976" (L.B.S. General From Oct. 1975 to Dec. 1978 File, Box: LBBC/S Files B. Irwin—Promotion, Archives of Heritage College and Seminary).

CHAPTER TWO

Gerald Benn   Marvin Brubacher

The first home of London Baptist Bible College & Seminary

and Theology, and Brubacher teaching courses in Greek, Bible, and Christian Education.[10]

At first, the school was based on the campus of Central Baptist Church, London, which was then located on the corner of Queens Avenue and Adelaide Street. The church's lead pastor was Robert Robinson, one of the men who had started the school and who served as the first vice chairman of the board. In order to pay his salary, Brubacher was hired as a full-time employee by Central Baptist Church with the understanding that he would work half-time with the church and half-time with the school. In addition to his role at the school, then, Brubacher was also responsible for Sunday School, Children's Church, Youth Ministry, Bus Ministry, and a Monday Night Bible Institute—the last of which he led with Benn, who was given a small stipend for serving in this area.[11]

The theological identity of LBS

The theological identity of the school consisted of four distinctives. First, it was evangelistic, with a desire to teach students to be soul-winners and "to establish local churches." Second, it was fundamentalist with a focus on "holiness and separation from apostasy." Third, it was baptistic, holding to "the primacy of Scripture and the priority of the local church." And fourth, it was premillennial, "emphasizing the pre-tribulational rapture as the blessed hope of the church."[12]

The doctrinal statement of the new school also provides an important window on the school's key convictions. Scripture was inerrant and marked by verbal, plenary inspiration. The school stood

---

10   Cleland, "Interview with Benn, Benn, and Barker, February 1, 2023"; *idem*, "Zoom interview with Brubacher, February 23, 2023."

11   Cleland, "Zoom interview with Brubacher, February 23, 2023."

12   "Canadian Baptist Bible College: Calendar 1976," p. 7 (Box: LBBC/S Catalogs '76–'93, Archives of Heritage College and Seminary).

against the charismatic movement that was a significant feature of the Christian world at the time: "We believe that the Holy Spirit endues men with gifts upon conversion, however, this school stands strongly opposed to the 'second work of grace' and the charismatic emphasis upon healing and speaking in tongues."[13] As for the person and work of Christ, there was a strong affirmation of his substitutionary atonement and second coming.[14] Christ will return to rapture believers and, in the words of the doctrinal statement, "set up the throne of David and establish His kingdom. His coming is imminent and will be pre-tribulational, and pre-millennial."[15]

The evangelical nature of the school was also clear in the statement on salvation and the Christian life. There was a call for people to "be born again" and an invitation to place one's faith in "God's Word" in order to receive "a new nature." A "personal faith in the Lord Jesus Christ" was emphasized as well as one's salvation being "eternally secure."[16] With regard to the Christian life, there was an insistence on the Christian to "walk in Christian love and holiness," and for his or her life to "be evidenced by sincere humility and genuine zeal for the advancement of the cause of Christ."[17]

The assertions regarding the church and baptism and the Lord's Supper clearly set forth the baptistic nature of the school. The local church was described as "a congregation of baptized believers" and baptism "the single immersion of a believer in water." This same

---

13 "Canadian Baptist Bible College: Calendar 1976," p. 12.

14 It is noteworthy that in an initial proposal for the doctrinal statement there was the statement that Jesus died for "our sins." This was crossed out and the phrase "the sins of the world" was substituted for it. Was there a concern that the phrase "our sins" could be interpreted as supporting particular redemption? See "Proposed Doctrinal Statement" (L.B.S. General From Oct. 1975 to Dec. 1978 File).

15 "Canadian Baptist Bible College: Calendar 1976," pp. 12–13.

16 "Canadian Baptist Bible College: Calendar 1976," p. 13.

17 "Canadian Baptist Bible College: Calendar 1976," p. 14.

baptism was to be the "pre-requisite to membership and privileges in a local church."[18]

And finally, the fundamentalist aspect of the school was most evident in the statement's assertions under the heading, "Biblical Separation." The overall importance of being separate from the world in order to be set apart for God was emphatically highlighted. In practice, this meant that all affiliation with apostasy was to be rejected. Thus, this section concluded: "The 20th century emphasis of ecumenical evangelism which involves apostates and evangelicals is to be denounced."[19] The ministry of an evangelist like Billy Graham would have been in view of what this statement called "ecumenical evangelism."

Students and programs

Regarding the school's expectations of the students, all of them were required to attend Central Baptist Church for at least four weeks before they were able to request to serve in another church. Engagement with Central Baptist involved participating in "Sunday School, Sunday Morning Worship Hour, Evening Worship Hour, and Wednesday Evening Prayer Service each week." There was also an expectation that students were believers and prepared to live according to "Christian standards of conduct."[20]

---

18 "Canadian Baptist Bible College: Calendar 1976," pp. 13–14.
19 "Canadian Baptist Bible College: Calendar 1976," p. 15.
20 "Canadian Baptist Bible College: Calendar 1976," p. 18.

"The influence of the godly male and female faculty members"
Mark Cuthbert

Mark Cuthbert

I began attending LBBC in it's second year. As I think back to those days, even though I can laugh at some of the arbitrary rules we had to keep, it was a season that impacted my life. In addition to learning discipline in a very structured setting, my future ministry was influenced the most by the relationships that were built and the Bible knowledge I gained in the classroom.

The relational side was clearly enhanced by the fact that I met my wife, Faith, at the school, and we both still have friends from those early days. In terms of Bible knowledge, the school placed a high value on learning Bible content. That knowledge provided a good foundation for my wife and I, as we both went on to complete graduate degrees at Grand Rapids Theological Seminary.

As I began my first pastorate in Brigden, Ontario, I

CHAPTER TWO

> was invited to teach part time at LBBC, taking the place of my father-in-law, Roly Smith, who had been teaching missions for a number of years. When a more qualified missions professor was hired, I continued teaching Bible Doctrine as an evening course.
>
> Clearly, the greatest impact the school made, came from the influence of the godly male and female faculty members who challenged the students to live lives fully devoted to the Lord.

In 1976 the school only offered a Bachelor of Theology and Bachelor of Religious Education.[21] By 1977, in addition to the undergraduate programs, the school had also initiated a three-year Graduate of Theology diploma in a Bible Institute Division, which was available for students to take without any educational prerequisites. There was also a new Graduate Division, which offered a Master of Divinity and a Master of Religious Education.[22] The Master of Divinity curriculum involved four Greek courses, two Hebrew courses, four systematic theology courses, three church history courses, and eight Bible electives. There were also courses in teaching and preaching methods, pastoral theology, and a variety of other practical and Christian education courses. Altogether, the program was 98 credit hours, with students taking between six and seven courses each semester.[23] These courses were in addition to attendance at the services mentioned

---

21 "Canadian Baptist Bible College: Calendar 1976," pp. 25–27.
22 "London Baptist Seminary 1977/1978," pp. 38–41 (Box: LBBC/S Catalogs '76–'93).
23 "London Baptist Seminary 1977/1978," p. 40.

above and were also to be taken alongside practical ministerial training. Such training was offered through the Christian Service Department where the dean of students offered students "opportunities for practical training and experience in supervised Christian service."[24]

Truth Aflame

The motto for the school was "Truth Aflame," which expressed the desire of the board that the school be marked by both truth and passion. Its theme verse was 2 Timothy 2:2, "And the things that thou has heard of me among many witnesses, the same commit thou to faithful men, who shall be able to teach others also" (KJV).[25] To disseminate this vision of LBS was the publication of *Truth Aflame*, which started as a quarterly magazine involving various pieces written by staff, faculty, and others connected to the school. The first issue appeared in November 1976.

A second issue came out in March 1977 and included school updates, an editorial, a section for pastors, praise and prayer requests, a section called "A Woman's Viewpoint," a spot to highlight students, and spaces for those ministering to youth, another for teachers, and another for ministering to children. It concluded with a note on upcoming events.

On the front page of the second issue of *Truth Aflame*, there was a column on three women who were a critical part of the school's staff in its early days. Marion Lankin was appointed as the dean of women, and also served as the dietitian and a missions teacher. Elsie Lawson was the bookkeeper and librarian, secretary, and "house mother in the ladies dormitory." Margaret Robinson served as the director of

---

24 "London Baptist Seminary 1977/1978," p. 18.
25 Marvin Brubacher, Letter to Stan Fowler, May 22, 1991, p. 2 (Articles Published RE: LBBC/S File, Box: LBBC/S Files B. Irwin—Promotion).

CHAPTER TWO

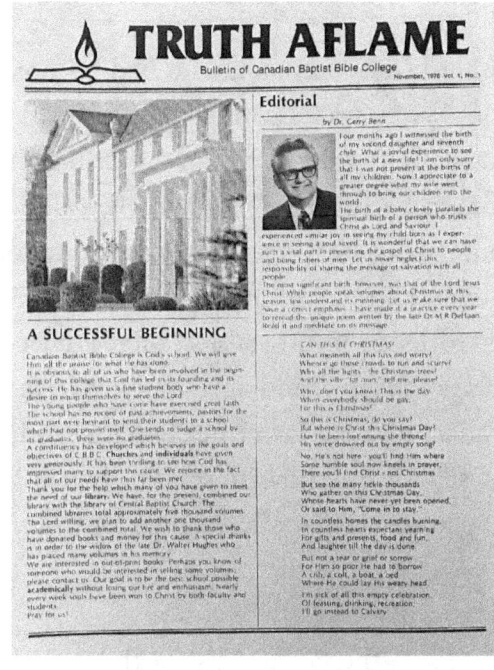

The first issue of *Truth Aflame*

Three female staff—Marion Lankin, Elsie Lawson, and Margaret Robinson

admissions and records.[26]

Elsie Lawson—the mother of Roy Lawson, who had become the FEBC general secretary in 1977—was an important figure in the early days of the London school. On the occasion of her retirement in 1980, there was a tribute to her in the *Truth Aflame*, calling her "Mom" Lawson. The tribute stated that she was "an inspiration to us all." She had a very influential role with the women of LBS and was praised for her desire to listen to others and offer advice. She was hard working, a woman of resolve, and an example of a fervent prayer. Her ministry had a lasting impact on the students, and even in her retirement from the school and move to seniors' housing, she aimed "to minister to the aged and shut-in in her own location."[27]

Student and faculty life

When the school began in 1976, there was a list of things that the student body was prohibited from participating in. The list included "the use of tobacco, alcoholic beverages, habit-forming drugs, playing with cards generally associated with gambling, and gambling in any form."[28] By 1979, the list had grown to include "dancing, attendance at movie theatres and membership in secret societies" as well as "the practice of those temporary Apostolic gifts generally associated with the Charismatic movement."[29] The concern with the Charismatic movement, seen both here and in the doctrinal statement, was very much in line with the majority opinion of Canadian Baptists in the twentieth century.[30] Informing this conviction was

---

26 "Meet Three Choice Women," *Truth Aflame* 1, no. 2 (March 1977), p. 1. For copies of *Truth Aflame*, see Truth Aflame File, Box: LBBC/S Files B. Irwin–Promotion.

27 "Tribute to 'Mom' Lawson," *Truth Aflame* 4, no. 5 (June 1980), pp. 7–8.

28 "Canadian Baptist Bible College: Calendar 1976," p. 18.

29 "London Baptist Seminary: 1979/1980," p. 20 (Box: LBBC/S Catalogs '76–'93).

30 For the Canadian Evangelical Baptist response to the Charismatic movement, see Ian Hugh Clary,

CHAPTER TWO

The faculty, staff, and student body in the fall of 1979.

a desire to be shaped by the Scriptures. As Canadian historian Ian Clary has commented more generally concerning the conviction of Arnold Dallimore and other fellow Canadian Baptists of the time: there was concern "that the objective content of the faith would be eroded by an emphasis on subjective experience."[31] In both conviction and practice, then, London called for its students to avoid the Charismatic movement.

The school had a number of cultural aspects that bespoke fundamentalism. Men were required to wear a shirt and tie, keep their hair cropped short, and were not permitted to sport any facial hair.

Reformed Evangelicalism and the Search for a Usable Past: The Historiography of Arnold Dallimore, Pastor-Historian (Göttingen: Vandenhoeck & Ruprecht, 2020), pp. 171–175.
31 Clary, *Reformed Evangelicalism and the Search for a Usable Past*, p. 174.

CHAPTER TWO

The King James Version (KJV) of the Bible was the only acceptable translation to be used.[32] Yet, alongside these aspects of fundamentalism, high teaching standards were set for the professors. David Barker, who joined the faculty in 1978, recalled teaching ten classes a semester, two classes a day. According to Benn, the school followed the advice of James Murray Grier—then on the faculty of Cedarville College and later dean of Grand Rapids Theological Seminary—who argued that a professor could either do well in the classroom or do well in writing. But a professor could not do both. Following this advice, LBS focused on excellence in teaching, and publishing, apart from *Truth Aflame*, was never a priority.[33]

"Life-moulding influence and instruction"
Mark Lowrie

Mark & Margaret Lowrie

I moved from Tennessee to pursue a Master's degree at London Baptist Seminary in 1978. Although a Canadian

---

32 Cleland, "Interview with Benn, Benn, and Barker, February 1, 2023."
33 Cleland, "Interview with Benn, Benn, and Barker, February 1, 2023."

> citizen, I had lived in the USA for nearly fifteen years. It was during those years I became a Christian. As I grew in the Lord, I sensed he was leading me to return to Canada for ministry. But since I had little knowledge of the Canadian evangelical climate, I felt I would benefit greatly from schooling in a Canadian context. I was not wrong. Studying under the professors and interacting with the growing student body not only built upon my theological foundation, but opened my eyes to the needs and opportunities in Canada. While at LBS I had the joy of writing the words to the school hymn. An even greater joy was meeting my future bride—Margaret Donald with whom I have been blessed in marriage and ministry partnership now for more than forty-four years. I thank God for the life-moulding influence and instruction I received at LBS.

Growth, a new location, and incorporation

In 1976 the school had but 37 students. Within two years, though, the student body had grown to 151. After another two years, the school numbered 217 students.[34] And by 1982, enrollment reached an all-time high of 225.[35] These years of growth were marked by excitement and financial success. As of the fiscal year end, June 1982, the school had an excess of $49,322.[36]

---

34 Gerry Benn, "Editor's Comments," *Truth Aflame* 6, no. 1 (October 1981), p. 2
35 Gerry Benn, "Editor's Comments," *Truth Aflame* 7, no. 2 (December 1982), p. 2.
36 Steve Field, "From the Business Manager," *Truth Aflame* 7, no. 1 (October 1982), p. 2.

Graduation day 1982

The school purchased its own building in 1980. The building, located at 30 Grand Avenue, had once been London Gospel Temple. The move was set for summer of 1981 and the goal was to raise $550,000 for the building along with another $50,000 for an updated library.[37] However, this move resulted in a falling-out between the leadership and Robert Robinson, the pastor at Central Baptist Church, where the school had been housed. Robinson was not at all happy with the relocation of the school and this led to a rift between him and the other board members. After LBS relocated to Grand Avenue, Robinson resigned from the board of the school.

When the school was meeting at Central, a number of houses had been bought for student housing. The move to the new location necessitated the purchase of an old apartment building that could serve as a dormitory for 118 students. The four-floor edifice was a block

---

37 Gerry Benn, "Editor's Comments," *Truth Aflame* 4, no. 4 (April 1980), p. 2.

CHAPTER TWO

The new building on Grand Avenue, London

away at 67 Grand Avenue. The student rooms were intended for single students who came from outside of London.[38] Not surprisingly, the work of moving to the new location took a lot of effort, and the jobs were often picked up by those connected to the faculty and staff. Liz Benn, Gerald Benn's wife, helped out in building maintenance, and in the new move, she helped clean the carpets of the school building, as well as working with other women to make curtains for the new apartments.[39]

Around the time of the school's relocation, it was incorporated. When the school had begun, its degrees had been granted through an affiliation with Piedmont College in North Carolina, since the school had not been given degree-granting status by the Ontario government. However, after a formal petition, the government made a policy change in 1980, which enabled the school to become incorporated and grant its own degrees. On June 17, 1981, the Government of

---

38 "New Dorm Facilities," *Truth Aflame* 5, no. 6 (August 1981), pp. 1, 3.
39 Cleland, "Interview with Benn, Benn, and Barker, February 1, 2023."

CHAPTER TWO

The new dorms

Ontario passed Private Bill 10 entitled, "An Act to Incorporate London Baptist Bible College and London Baptist Seminary." This was a clear answer to prayer and an important milestone in the school's history. Henceforth, it would be called London Baptist Bible College and London Baptist Seminary (LBBC/S), the former connected to its undergraduate programs and the latter to the graduate programs.[40]

Challenges and Benn's resignation

After this significant period of growth, however, the school began to decline in terms of student numbers. The enrolment in 1983 was 215 students, a decrease of 10 from the previous year.[41] The following year, 1984, the enrollment numbers began to be far less frequently listed in school programs and in *Truth Aflame*. By the spring of 1986

---

40 "London Baptist Seminary Incorporated by the Province of Ontario," *Truth Aflame* 5, no. 6 (August 1981), pp. 1–2.
41 "London Baptist Bible College Begins Year Eight with Enrolment of 215 Students," *Truth Aflame* 8, no. 1 (October 1983), p. 1.

there was evident concern about the decreased enrollment as well as a concomitant decrease in giving to the general budget. The school was faced with a potential deficit of $50,000.[42]

In a presidential letter that Benn issued at the time, he presented the two main causes for this lower enrollment: first, there was a lack of people college age, and second, men were deterred from entering the ministry on account of a desire to earn more in other professions.[43] By the fall of 1987, there were only 148 students.[44] This change was evidently felt personally by Benn in his role as president.

In June of 1987, West Park Baptist Church approached Benn to see if he would be interested in serving as their senior pastor. His initial response was to ask them to look elsewhere, but in the case that no one was found, they could approach him again. And so they did, in October of 1987. As he shared this journey with the board on November 24, 1987, he reflected on the difficulties at London. He wrote, "wouldn't it be great to be out from under the great financial burden at L.B.B.C., the need to vigorously recruit new students each year, and the need to be on the road making contacts." He went on, "These reasons and the prospect of a better salary did appeal to my carnal nature." Despite the allure to go somewhere else, as of November, Benn had resolved to stay at LBBC/S.[45]

Although Benn was initially hesitant about leaving to go to West Park, this London church continued to pursue Benn as their future pastor. Eventually, Benn felt a peace that his move away from

---

42 Steve Field, "From the Business Manager," *Truth Aflame* (Spring 1986), p. 8.

43 Gerry Benn, Letter "From the President's Desk," March 1986. This letter was attached to the Spring 1986 issue of *Truth Aflame*.

44 Gerry Benn, "Year Twelve Begins," *Truth Aflame* (Fall 1987), p. 2. The body of the text says 147 students, but based on the graph, the number seems to be 148.

45 Gerry Benn, Letter to the Board, November 24, 1987 (Board of Governors 1987 File, Box: LBBC/S Files B. Irwin Board of Governors Board Committees).

CHAPTER TWO

Tribute To Dr. Benn

On Monday, May 16, 1988, our faithful and beloved President, Dr. Benn, announced his resignation from L.B.B.C./S. Dr. Benn was born in Wallaceburg, Ontario, and at age seventeen trusted Christ as Saviour. Immediately, he sensed God's call on his life. He graduated from London College of Bible and Missions, Columbia Bible College, Windsor Teacher's College, Tennessee Temple University, and from Bob Jones University with a Ph.D. in Christian Education. He taught at Tennessee Temple University for six years, and in 1976 responded to an invitation from the first Board of Directors of L.B.B.C./S. to become the founding President.

Dr. Benn served as President for twelve years, and distinguished himself among his students as an effective teacher, a compassionate leader, and a spiritual giant. For those of us who worked with him, we found him to be, in addition to the man of God known by the students, a man of principle and determination, committed to the school in both its distinctives and concern for its success, and personally interested in each of us as a true friend.

We also express our tribute to his wife, Liz, who, in both her formal and casual involvements with the school, brought color and joy, spiritual maturity, and a model of dedication to her husband in his intense ministry for the school.

We honour Dr. Benn for his years of service at L.B.B.C./S. His leadership and vision as he guided us through the early years of establishing a school, his commitment to the mission of the school as we became established and more developed in our programming, and his spiritual vitality as he directed us in our walk with God and guided us through some difficult times, will long be remembered as some of the notable marks of Dr. Benn's ministry as President.

We pray God's richest blessing as Dr. and Mrs. Benn begin their ministry at West Park Baptist Church. We know that this privileged people will enjoy all the benefits we have enjoyed from these choice servants of Christ.

A tribute to Dr Benn

LBBC/S was the right step. At the May 16, 1988, board meeting, Benn's resignation letter was read, which stated that he would finish at LBBC/S as of June 30, 1988. The minutes stated that the move had to do with Benn's following God's call on his life and was not in any way a dismissal. Benn was leaving for a new ministry, and the board was supportive of this change.[46]

> ## "London's commitment to the local church"
> Rick Buck
>
> I had the privilege of attending London Baptist Bible College in the BTh program, and then later attending London Seminary to complete my MDiv degree. My early years at London were instrumental in developing my love of God's Word as it was central to every class I took, whether it was a Bible, theology, or practical ministry course.
>
>
> **Rick Buck**
>
> The professors made a lasting imprint on my life and ministry. Godly men like Dr. Dave Barker and Dr. Doug Schmidt poured into my life, not only in the classroom, but in showing me practically what godly pastoral

---

46 "London Baptist Bible College and London Baptist Seminary, Meeting of the Board of Governors, Monday, May 16, 1988," p. 1 (Board of Governors 1988 File, Box: LBBC/S Files B. Irwin Board of Governors Board Committees).

> ministry looked like. The school's smaller size meant that our teachers had time to invest in the lives of their students and my profs became my mentors.
>
> London's commitment to the local church developed in me a desire to serve Christ's church, and working alongside profs and fellow students helped me to develop leadership and pastoral skills that I was able to carry forward to over three decades of pastoral ministry. I am so grateful for the foundation that helped to nurture in me a deeper passion for Christ and His church and service for the gospel.

Following Benn's resignation, *Truth Aflame* included an article dedicated to "our faithful and beloved President" and his ministry at the school. Benn was remembered "as an effective teacher, a compassionate leader, and a spiritual giant." The entry went on to highlight him as a "man of God … a man of principle and determination, committed to the school in both its distinctives and concern for its success, and personally interested in each of us as a true friend." The article also highlighted the involvement of his wife Liz in the school, who "brought color and joy, spiritual maturity, and a model of dedication to her husband in his intense ministry for the school." The article concluded by thanking Benn for his years of service and blessing him as he went to serve at West Park.[47]

From Benn to Barker to Brubacher

Following Benn's resignation, the school was faced with the need to

---

47 "Tribute to Dr. Benn," *Truth Aflame* (Fall 1988), p. 2.

CHAPTER TWO

Dr Barker in his element

CHAPTER TWO

Dave Barker in his office with Glen Francis (MDiv 1988)

fill the role of president. In June of 1988, David Barker agreed to fill the position of acting president.

At the time, Barker was serving as the Academic Dean of the Seminary. However, Barker's transition to acting president was made with the caveat that it was "until a new president is in office."[48] Barker was willing to undertake the role, but he made it clear that it would be in a temporary, interim capacity.[49] Barker served in this role from the spring of 1988 until January 1990, at which point Marvin Brubacher returned to the school in order to serve as president.

Brubacher had left the school in 1981 to serve full-time in pastoral ministry at Faith Baptist Church in St. Thomas until 1989.

---

48 "London Baptist Bible College and London Baptist Seminary, Meeting of the Board of Governors, Monday, June 6, 1988" (Board of Governors 1988 File).
49 Cleland, "Interview with Benn, Benn, and Barker, February 1, 2023."

CHAPTER TWO

The faculty, staff, and students of LBBC/S in 1990

Brubacher was hesitant to return to the school, and he was not the school's first choice. However, Brubacher believed he should respond to the school's invitation after several important conversations with his wife, his extended family, and the elders at his church, Faith Baptist.[50] In the November 1989 board meeting minutes, there occurs the following statement about Brubacher's decision to return to the school: "Brubacher expressed his thanks to God for His direction." Even though it was hard for him to leave his church at the close of 1989, he felt a distinct peace about going back to the school.[51]

---

50 Cleland, "Zoom interview with Brubacher, February 23, 2023," and Marvin Brubacher, Email to Jonathan N. Cleland, August 9, 2023.

51 "London Baptist Bible College and London Baptist Seminary, Meeting of the Board of Governors, Monday, November 27, 1989," p. 1 (Board of Governors 1989 File, Box: LBBC/S Files B. Irwin Board of Governors Board Committees).

CHAPTER TWO

To change or not to change

During the entire history of LBBC/S, its relationship with the FEBC was tense and somewhat unclear. While a majority of those at the school wished to cultivate this relationship, there were some who desired a stronger degree of independence. In the summer of 1985, *Truth Aflame* included a graph of the denominational affiliations of the graduates for that school year. 72% were connected to FEBC. However, along with 7% from Associated Gospel Churches and 10% being from "Other," the next largest group was comprised of 11% who came from churches described as "Unaffiliated Baptist."[52] Evidently there was a contingency, both in leadership but also in the student body, that continued to desire independence from the FEBC.

But the school and the times were changing, and a shift can be seen through the school's ongoing relationship with the Fellowship of Evangelical Baptist Theological Education Committee (FEBTEC). Although the school was not initially a part of FEBTEC, and thus not an official school of FEBC, in 1987 the question was raised at the board level as to whether it should be. That February, the board decided that the school should not be directly involved with the FEBTEC.[53] A year later in February 1988, though, this question was raised again at the board. Again, it was decided, however, that the school should not join FEBTEC out of concern that it could "in some way interfere with the autonomy of Baptist schools."[54] Nevertheless, on February 9, 1989, the board rescinded its earlier position and voted to join FEBTEC.[55] However, as the notes from this meeting show,

---

52 Gerry Benn, "Editor's Comments," *Truth Aflame* (Summer 1985), p. 2.
53 "London Baptist Bible College and London Baptist Seminary, Meeting of the Board of Governors, Thursday, February 26, 1987," p. 1 (Board of Governors 1987 File).
54 Gerry Benn, Letter to Roy Lawson, February 25, 1988, p. 1 (Board of Governors 1988 File).
55 "Fellowship of Evangelical Baptist Theological Education Committee, Tuesday, February 28, 1989," p. 2 (Board of Governors 1989 File).

at least one member of the board was not happy with this decision.⁵⁶

Along with this move towards a more direct connection with the FEBC, the dynamics of the school were changing in other areas as well. At the December 8, 1992, board meeting, there was a motion to adapt the Community Life Commitment, specifically by removing the prohibition stating that students of the school could not attend movie theatres. There was a lively discussion around the topic, yet the motion was moved and seconded. More discussion followed. Finally, it was brought to a vote. The minutes stated, "The vote proceeded with 4 in favour, 5 opposed, and 4 abstentions. The motion was defeated."⁵⁷ Such a varied outcome shows the divide that was growing between those who wanted to see the school change in significant ways and those who wished to stay true to the fundamentalist roots of the school.

Pushing this pressure to change were the financial difficulties besetting the school. In a letter dated June 11, 1992, there was explicit mention of these significant financial challenges. It stated in no uncertain terms, "Unless the Lord intervenes, this year's deficit will approach $180,000." However, when the school's Advisory Council was asked how they felt about the school, six were very supportive, nine very concerned, and four were somewhat concerned. For some, there was an agreement that the school had "reached a better balance." Yet others on this council felt that there had been a compromising of the school's identity and original vision. In the words of the letter:

> The School is perceived to have moved too far from its

---

56 "London Baptist Bible College and London Baptist Seminary, Meeting of the Board of Governors, Thursday, February 9, 1989," p. 1 (Board of Governors 1989 File).

57 "London Baptist Bible College and London Baptist Seminary, Meeting of the Board of Governors, Tuesday, December 8, 1992," pp. 6–7 (Board of Governors 1992 File, Box: LBBC/S Files B. Irwin Board of Governors Board Committees).

roots and distinctiveness. ... Some of the School's most committed supporters fear that our loss of Baptistic emphasis, independence from the Fellowship, and lowering of lifestyle convictions have resulted in LBBC becoming just another Fellowship school.[58]

By the summer of 1992, then, it was clear that the school and its constituency were divided. There were serious financial difficulties, and there were some who wanted to move toward a greater relationship with the FEBC, while others believed that this very move would distance the school too greatly from its historical foundation. If the school was to simply become "just another Fellowship school," then it would open up the possibility of having one united school instead of two Ontario FEBC schools in competition with each other. As we will see in the next chapter, this would be the journey LBBC/S would embark on in the summer of 1992. As we shall see, from the summer of 1992 to the summer of 1993, Brubacher would work with Stanley Fowler, the acting president at Central, to bring about a union of Central and LBBC/S.

An ending and a new beginning

Although the London faculty did not publish much throughout its history, one particular publication points to what yet lay ahead. In the autumn of 1991, Michael A.G. Haykin, professor of church history at Central Baptist Seminary, published the first edition of a new journal entitled *The Baptist Review of Theology/La Révue Baptiste de Théologie*.[59] It was Haykin's desire "that this journal will help

---

58   June 11, 1992, Advisory Council Letter, p. 1 (Advisory Council File, Box: LBBC/S Files B. Irwin Board of Governors Board Committees).
59   The journal ran from 1991–1998, publishing a total of eight volumes.

to meet a genuine need on the Canadian theological scene, namely, to provide a forum for theological thinking and reflection from an evangelical Baptist perspective."[60] A little less than two years later, in the spring of 1993, the London professor of Bible, David Barker, wrote an article for this journal—"Praise and Praxis: Doxology as the Context for Kingdom Ministry."[61] Barker's article is important on a historical level for several reasons. For one, it is a collaboration between Central and London, with Haykin (Central) overseeing Barker's (London) publication. Second, it appeared in spring 1993, and was the last time Barker used the affiliation of "London Baptist Seminary, London, Ontario"[62] — the merger documents were signed on March 27, 1993, and by the fall of 1993, Barker's affiliation had been changed to Heritage Baptist College and Seminary. Third, the content of Barker's essay is *apropos* for the final year of London's existence. In the conclusion to the article, Barker wrote:

> Kingdom life and ministry does not readily yield its praise to God. But, in spite of the struggle, we must be called back to the foundational scriptural truth captured in the *Westminster Catechism*, "the chief end of man is to glorify God, and to enjoy him forever." The first and last word of the Christian faith is a doxological word—"Hallelujah!"[63]

If there is one thought that captures the history of LBBC/S, from its beginnings in 1976 to its conclusion in 1993, it is praise for God's

---

60 Michael A.G. Haykin, "Introduction," *The Baptist Review of Theology/La Révue Baptiste de Théologie* 1, no. 1 (Autumn 1991), p. 1.

61 David G. Barker, "Praise and Praxis: Doxology as the Context for Kingdom Ministry," *The Baptist Review of Theology/La Révue Baptiste de Théologie* 3, no. 1 (Spring 1993), pp. 4–17.

62 Barker, "Praise and Praxis," p. 17.

63 Barker, "Praise and Praxis," p. 14.

CHAPTER TWO

faithfulness. The school went through a lot in its brief history—rapid student growth, a substantial physical move in London, financial loss, and disparate visions. Yet it also was a place where Canadian students were trained for a lifetime of ministry, many of whom continue to serve faithfully in churches and occupy significant leadership roles to this day.

The spring of 1993 brough an era to a close. Lying ahead was a new school where Central and London, once rivals, would come together—a school where men like Barker and Haykin would serve together on the same faculty. It is to the merger of these two schools, and the history of Heritage, that we now turn.

3

"An enterprise of faith": A history of Heritage Baptist College and Theological Seminary, 1993–2023

Merging two schools

With both schools struggling financially and facing a decrease in enrollment, Marvin Brubacher, president of LBBC/S, and Stanley Fowler, acting president of CBS, knew that something needed to change. At a conference in the summer of 1992 the two met together and discussed the possibility of a merger of the two schools. Both men agreed that a merger was necessary for the future longevity of the schools, but they also knew it would not be easy to bring the schools together. When Fowler first talked to the CBS board about doing the merger, one member remarked, "Donkeys will fly before you pull that off." As it turned out, Brubacher and Fowler were about to see donkeys fly![1]

---

1   Jonathan N. Cleland, "Zoom interview with Marvin Brubacher," February 23, 2023.

CHAPTER THREE

There were two major hurdles standing in the way of a merger. First, there was the issue of theological differences. A key marker of LBBC/S' history and identity was its commitment to a premillennial dispensational eschatology; this was not, however, the stance of Central. Central had a more open position, allowing for a diversity of views on eschatology. The question was, then, what the stance of the school would be, should the merger happen. Second, there was the question of the school's location. Many FEBC churches were based in Toronto, yet Central, although based just north of Toronto in Gormley, did not really have a good location. LBBC/S, on the other hand, was based in London and had future plans for relocation to a better site in the city.[2]

The question of where the school would be located was solved quickly. CBS from the start was willing to sell what they owned and relocate to London.[3] In addition, the school would offer some "extension courses" out of a church in Toronto.[4] Thus, the main issue to be resolved concerned the school's doctrinal stance. At an October meeting of the LBBC/S Amalgamation Committee, there was a proposal that the new school would be premillennial, but would allow for both a historic premillennial position and a dispensational premillennial position. Moreover, there would be a caveat that the board members and faculty would sign an annual document declaring that they would not teach against such a position, though they would not need to hold to it personally.[5] Despite this attempt, the desire for the

---

2 Jonathan N. Cleland, "Zoom interview with Marvin Brubacher," March 10, 2023.
3 "London Baptist Bible College and London Baptist Seminary, Meeting of the Board of Governors, Tuesday, August 18, 1992," p. 3 (Board of Governors 1992 File, Box: LBBC/S Files B. Irwin Board of Governors Board Committees, Archives of Heritage College and Seminary).
4 "Fellowship Baptist Seminaries merge to absorb recessionary cost," *Hallelujah* 6, no. 2, Spring 1993 (Articles Published RE: LBBC/S File, Box: LBBC/S Files B. Irwin—Promotion, Archives of Heritage College and Seminary).
5 "LBBC/S Amalgamation Committee," Oct 13, 1992 (Board of Governors 1992 File).

school to be premillennial was not supported by CBS' constituency.

In order to facilitate a merger, then, Fowler and Brubacher put together a merger committee involving the boards from both schools. The board alternated the chair; one meeting the chair was from LBBC/S, the next from CBS. Through much prayer, discussion, and deliberation in this committee, another solution was presented on how to deal with the question of theology. The school would be open on the position of eschatology, allowing for a variety of different views. However, during the first two years of the school there would be a mandatory eschatology course in which the dispensational premillennial view was to be respectfully and carefully taught by Brubacher himself. This proved to be a reasonable way forward, and although there were constituencies connected to both schools that were not fully persuaded by the notion of a merger, LBBC/S and CBS agreed to amalgamate.[6]

A meeting of both boards took place on January 9, 1993.[7] On February 15 congregations affiliated with Central voted 90 to 4 in favour of the merger, and on February 23 LBBC/S' board agreed unanimously to the merger.[8] The legal merger then happened on March 27, 1993.

The new school was to be called Heritage Baptist College and Heritage Theological Seminary. Brubacher served as the first president and Fowler as the academic dean. The first school year began in September 1993 with a total of 238 students—177 students in the college and 61 in the seminary.[9] In a Christian news article written

---

6   Cleland, "Zoom interview with Brubacher," March 10, 2023.
7   Marvin Brubacher, "EXTRA! EXTRA!" *LBBC/S Priority Post*, 1993, p. 1 (Priority Post Permanent Copies File, Box: LBBC/S Files B. Irwin — Promotion).
8   Doug Koop, "Baptist Bible colleges prepare to merge," *Christian Week*, March 16, 1993 (Articles Published RE: LBBC/S File).
9   Marvin Brubacher, "Heritage Begins!" and "The Heritage Student," *Heritage Priority Post* 1993 [pt.

CHAPTER THREE

The boards of LBBC/S and CBS.

ChristianWeek is your "window on Christian faith and life in Canada." Read it to stay in touch with important stories on the Church in Canada and the impact of Christian witness upon Canadian life.

A window on Christian faith and life in Canada   March 16, 1993

Baptist Bible colleges prepare to merge

Realizing that "there is nothing other than history to keep us apart," two southern Ontario Bible training centres are merging before the next school year.

LONDON, ON
By Doug Koop
ChristianWeek staff

By the time school opens next September, London Baptist Bible College and Central Baptist Seminary/Bible College, now located in Gormley (north of Toronto), will be one institution.

The formal decision to merge the two independent Baptist schools was approved February 15 by a 90-4 vote of delegates at a special meeting of congregations affiliated with Central, and unanimously by London's governing board on February 23.

London president Marvin Brubacher has been appointed president of the new institution and chairman of the steering committee finalizing details of the merger.

The merged schools, which will be known as Heritage Baptist College and Heritage Theological Seminary, will at least initially be located at the London campus. Extension courses will be offered in the Toronto area previously served by Central.

Leaders of the two schools believe the merger is good stewardship of human and financial resources. "God used the financial issue to make us ask the serious questions," says Brubacher. "We believe it would please God for us to have a unified school, and that it will capture the hearts and minds of our constituency."

Constituency concerns

Stan Fowler, who has been serving as interim president at Central, identifies two primary reasons for the merger. "The Evangelical Baptist constituency in Ontario is not large enough to support two quality schools," he says.

Both of the present schools are recognized by the Theological Education Board of the Fellowship of Evangelical Baptist Churches in Canada. Although their primary orientation is toward Fellowship Baptist churches, each school serves students from other denominations as well.

A second factor, says Fowler, who will be dean of the merged schools' seminary division, "has been the growing recognition that things that have divided the schools in the past are not serious enough to keep us apart. We realized that there is nothing other than history to keep us apart."

London Bible College was formed in 1976 with a distinctive emphasis on premillenial dispensationalism. The doctrinal statements of the merged schools will have a more open statement on eschatology. "Our particular heritage of premillenialism will be maintained through a required course," says Brubacher.

"This is a positive move forward on the part of Baptists in Ontario," says Fowler. "By finding ways to stay together rather than apart, our institutions are catching up to where our congregations have been for some time already."

A Look Inside
Noise and neighbors 2
Mossop verdict 4
Multi-faith witness 8-9
The Spring Collection ... 10-18

The lead article in *Christian Week*, March 16, 1993

CHAPTER THREE

on the merger, Fowler offered two insights into why the merger was necessary. First, because Ontario was not large enough to warrant two high quality FEBC schools. And the second reason, Fowler observed, was "the growing recognition that the things that have divided the schools in the past are not serious enough to keep us apart. We realized that there is nothing other than history to keep us apart."[10]

The new location

When Heritage started in London in the fall of 1993, it was the intent that a new school building would be constructed by 1994. A London location was set and everything was ready for building. However, due to a plan to expand the boundaries of the city of London—initiated by the province of Ontario—the place where Heritage was set to be was in a zone that would not be open for building in the near future. Due to the deteriorating conditions of the building on Grand Avenue, however, the leadership knew the school needed to relocate. They looked for other locations in London but there were no options that worked.[11] Seeing that nothing was available in London, there was a new interest in addressing the problem of location that had been faced in the considerations leading up to the merger. Since there was a desire to be closer to Toronto, the idea was that the school should relocate somewhere east of London. In addition to this, they also wanted something close to Highway 401—the main highway through Southern Ontario—that had both an existing building that could be used for academic purposes as well as room for further expansion if

---

2], p. 1–2 (Priority Post Permanent Copies File).

10 Koop, "Baptist Bible colleges prepare to merge."

11 Cleland, "Zoom interview with Brubacher," March 10, 2023. Reflecting on the situation, Brubacher commented that if they had waited for the location in London, they would have had to wait for "nearly a decade." Marvin Brubacher, Email to Jonathan N. Cleland, August 24, 2023.

CHAPTER THREE

The new building in Cambridge, ON

need be.[12]

Through the aid of a real estate agent, the school was introduced to a building on Holiday Inn Drive in Cambridge. The building had been on the market for some time and was being sold by Encyclopedia Britannica Canada. The location was perfect, close to the highway, close to bus stops, and roughly halfway between London and Toronto.[13] In two editions of the *Priority Post*, which was the publication that took over after LBBC/S' *Truth Aflame*, there is a helpful amount of detail about the purchase and the eventual move of the school to the new location. The purchase, renovations, and move to the new building all happened very quickly.

In April 1994, the board initially agreed to look into purchasing the property. The board made an offer in May, and Britannica agreed with three conditions that needed to be met. First, the board had to agree to terms of purchase by September 1. Then, the "two other conditions involved obtaining a necessary rezoning by-law and a positive environmental assessment."[14] The first condition was met on August 27, when the board unanimously agreed to purchase the

---

12 Cleland, "Zoom interview with Brubacher," March 10, 2023; Brubacher, Email to Cleland, August 24, 2023.
13 Cleland, "Zoom interview with Brubacher," March 10, 2023.
14 *Priority Post* 3, no. 1 (December 1994), p. 1 (Priority Post Permanent Copies File).

property. The following two conditions were soon met as well. As the *Priority Post* described the process:

> During the fall, Heritage has worked closely with the Cambridge Planning Department and Britannica to satisfy the requirements of the rezoning process and the policies of the Ministry of Environment and Energy. One of the stipulations was that an archaeological assessment be conducted. We were thankful that this study revealed nothing of historical significance on the property. On Monday, November 21, 1994, the Planning and Development Committee of the City of Cambridge voted unanimously to recommend to City Council that the Heritage rezoning application be approved. City Council did just that on November 28, 1994. The final condition has also been satisfied with the receipt of verbal clearance from the Environment Ministry with regard to potential building and/or site contamination. Throughout the process, the mayor, the City Council, and all of the future neighbours of Heritage have been extremely supportive of our plan.[15]

The initial closing date was set for the end of December 1994. However, this purchase date was pushed back to April 28, 1995 due to an environmental issue that needed to be resolved. From then until July the building underwent an extensive renovation and the first summer intensive class started on August 7. By April, the full amount needed to purchase the building—$1.9 million— was obtained through donation pledges and the sale of the building in

---

15 *Priority Post* 3, no. 1 (December 1994), p. 2.

CHAPTER THREE

Tours of the new facility

CHAPTER THREE

The new dorms

London.[16]

Initially, students were going to live at the Holiday Inn across the street, but this plan fell through at the last minute. Thus, the next project that was taken on immediately was the building of two dorms. The building of these residences was done by the late fall of 1995 and students moved into them on November 10, 1995.[17]

In a story written for the *Cambridge Times*, Brubacher reflected on the move: "We've looked in Kitchener and Waterloo, but this site is exactly what we've been looking for." He continued, "I don't anticipate that we'll ever outgrow this new campus. In real terms, it doubles the

---

16 "Cambridge—Here We Come!" *Priority Post* 3, no. 2 (June 1995), p. 4. (Priority Post Permanent Copies File).
17 Cleland, "Zoom interview with Brubacher," March 10, 2023.

space we've had available to us ... This new campus creates the image we've always felt we deserved."[18]

In reflecting on the move to Cambridge, Brubacher also recalled the many miraculous stories of things aligning in order for the purchase to happen. Not only did Britannica amazingly reduce their asking price from $3.8 million to $1.9 million, but the money to purchase the building was donated in a little over a year. Moreover, a significant amount of the money came in close to the deadline, including the sale of the building in London and a $90,000 donation coming in just days before the closing. As Brubacher commented, "The whole thing, from start to end, was a gift from God."[19]

The 1990s

From 1993–2000, the school experienced good numbers in terms of both enrollment and financial support. In February 1997, the school started working toward building the Heritage Community Centre to support the large number of incoming students. By the winter semester of 1997, the school registered 290 students.[20] The ground-breaking ceremony for the Community Centre was held on August 8, 1997, and after the 1997–1998 school year, the bible college and seminary "ended their operations in the black for the fifth year."[21] That September on the 26th of the month, 1998, the Community Centre was dedicated.[22]

---

18 Ray Martin, "First classes start in a few weeks: Bible college prepares for move to Cambridge," *The Cambridge Times* (Saturday, July 29, 1995), p. 9 (Articles Published RE: LBBC/S File).

19 Cleland, "Zoom interview with Brubacher," March 10, 2023.

20 "President's Annual Report, Presented to the Board of Directors at the Annual Celebration, September 27, 1997," pp. 2–3 (President's Annual Reports [Annual Meetings] File, Box: President Brubacher Archive 2, Archives of Heritage College and Seminary).

21 "President's Annual Report, Presented to the Board of Directors at the Annual Celebration, September 26, 1998," pp. 2–3 (President's Annual Reports [Annual Meetings] File).

22 "President's Annual Report, Presented to the Board of Directors at the Annual Celebration, Sep-

CHAPTER THREE

The building of the Community Centre

And at the close of the 1999–2000 academic year, due to a gift of $441,000, the school finished the year with a $457,559 surplus.[23]

These years of Heritage's history well display the expansion and fruitful ministry of the school. One student, Theresa Beach (neé Keddy), described her positive experience of being a student during these years. She initially enrolled in the one-year certificate program in 1997. Yet, like many other students, after she felt a calling into ministry, she decided to enter into the Bachelor of Religious Education program, from which she graduated in 2001. During her time as a student, Theresa also met Mark Beach, a fellow student, and the two of them married in October 2001. In addition to being a student, Theresa worked at Heritage from 1998–2001, and this involvement in the school continued into the 2000s. She left for a period, returning in 2009 for a short time as the admissions co-ordinator before becoming the registrar in 2010. Meanwhile, her husband, Mark, has

---

tember 28, 1999," p. 2 (President's Annual Reports [Annual Meetings] File).

23 "President's Annual Report, Presented to the Board of Directors at the Annual Celebration, September 26, 2000," p. 2 (President's Annual Reports [Annual Meetings] File).

CHAPTER THREE

Mark and Theresa Beach

Staff, students, and faculty, 1997/1998

CHAPTER THREE

served in a variety of different ministerial contexts.[24]

Theresa and Mark offer one example of students who attended Heritage during this time. More than just faculty, boards, presidents, and buildings, the history of Heritage involves the stories of students like the Beaches. Students being taught and equipped for the sake of Christ and his ministry in the world. Mark and Theresa remind us of this lasting legacy of the school from the 1990s.

"The foundation for my present-day ministry"
Aaron Groat

Aaron Groat

First, it was the excitement of something fresh and new! I attended my first year of Heritage in London as I thought my dreams for seminary would take me south of the border. In chatting with Dr. Fowler, though, it became apparent that Heritage was ideal to prepare me for local pastoral ministry. Commuting to finish my degree at the new campus in Cambridge wasn't easy, but there was a sense that God was positioning this school to be used to prepare Christian leaders for service at home

---

24 Jonathan N. Cleland, "Zoom interview with Theresa Beach," May 9, 2023.

and around the world.

Second, one of my fondest memories played out after classes in the seminary lounge. Theology was often hammered out within the student community. We could discuss and disagree on what we were learning. There was freedom to share life over a meal as we grew in our ministry preparation. Professors would often join in the conversation, demonstrate genuine care and concern for our development. The relationships I began at the seminary continue to this day.

My time at Heritage laid the foundation for my present-day ministry. I am very thankful to God for providing Heritage Seminary.

Heritage on the international stage

Following the 1990s, the school entered into a major controversy, not only within the FEBC, but one that was swirling within North American evangelicalism more broadly. In 2001, Heritage's New Testament Professor, William J. Webb published his book *Slaves, Women & Homosexuals: Exploring the Hermeneutics of Cultural Analysis* that he had been working on since 1995 or so. The book was an argument for the use of what Webb called the Redemptive-Movement Hermeneutic (RMH), that is, a specific hermeneutic for reading and applying the teaching of the Bible in such controverted areas as women in ministry. Employing this hermeneutic, Webb concluded the book with a statement that the position he termed "complementary egalitarian"—a position that affirmed the place of women in all areas of

CHAPTER THREE

church ministry—was the view that he found preferable.²⁵ As outlined in the book's "Acknowledgments," Webb noted that the book was "a journey of five years with fellow faculty members." He described his coworkers as "cordial and caring even when expressing points of significant disagreement." Moreover, this work, he explained, was produced in light of the encouragement from the administration, the board, and the president. Yet, he also offered a disclaimer: "My views, of course, do not represent any official seminary position; a variety of perspectives are represented at Heritage in an atmosphere of gracious deference and mutual respect."²⁶

In 2002 a number of reviews of the book appeared. One longer, more detailed review article was published by Thomas R. Schreiner, professor of New Testament at The Southern Baptist Theological Seminary. Schreiner argued that Webb's "defense of egalitarianism is found lacking, for he fails to establish his case exegetically or hermeneutically."²⁷ In addition to these academic reviews, the school was hearing a lot of feedback about the book. Some were emailing the school to express their appreciation for Webb being allowed to speak openly. Others, however, lamented that the school allowed for the publication in the first place and expressed deep concern for where the school might be theologically.²⁸

One particularly noteworthy case had to do with a paper written by the research assistant of Pastor James MacDonald—the senior

---

25 William J. Webb, *Slaves, Women & Homosexuals: Exploring the Hermeneutics of Cultural Analysis* (Downers Grove, IL: InterVarsity Press, 2001), p. 250.

26 Webb, *Slaves, Women & Homosexuals*, p. 11.

27 Thomas R. Schreiner, "William J. Webb's *Slaves, Women & Homosexuals*: A Review Article," *The Southern Baptist Journal of Theology* 6, no. 1 (2002), p. 64. Webb later responded to Schreiner's article: William J. Webb, "The Limits of a Redemptive-Movement Hermeneutic: A Focused Response to T.R. Schreiner," *Evangelical Quarterly* 75, no. 4 (2003), pp. 327–342.

28 For these correspondences, see "Bill Webb's Book and other related issues File," Box: President Brubacher Archive 1, Archives of Heritage College and Seminary.

pastor at the time of the Harvest Bible Chapel in Rolling Hills, Illinois—which Wayne Grudem of Phoenix Seminary had asked to be written. This paper was connected to Grudem's concern about the book and MacDonald's concern for the school. MacDonald had a personal interest in the school since he had graduated from LBBC/S. MacDonald personally called Brubacher in March of 2002, expressing his concern regarding how the school had shifted from the fundamentalist convictions of LBBC/S to the more open stance of Heritage.[29] Brubacher responded to this concern of MacDonald's by pointing out the desire of the school to graciously present the variety of evangelical perspectives on different views, including the question of women in ministry.[30]

Of all the responses to Webb's book, the most scathing interaction came from Wayne Grudem himself. At the Annual Meeting of the Evangelical Theological Society in November 2003, Grudem delivered a paper entitled "Does Our Culture Sometimes Reflect a 'Better Ethic' than the Bible? An Analysis of William Webb's 'Redemptive Movement Hermeneutic.'"[31] Following the conference, Grudem published the paper as a book review in the *Journal of the Evangelical Theological Society* (JETS) in 2004. The normal length of reviews in this journal is a few pages. Grudem's review was forty-eight pages long! His conclusion was clear: according to him, Webb did not offer an acceptable hermeneutic for reading the Bible.[32]

---

29 Marvin Brubacher, "Notes on MacDonald phone call, March 26, 2002" ("Bill Webb's Book and other related issues File").

30 Marvin Brubacher, "Letter response to MacDonald, April 7, 2002" ("Bill Webb's Book and other related issues File").

31 "Jesus Christ is the Same Yesterday, Today & Forever: Evangelical Theological Society: 55th Annual Meeting," Program, November 19–21, 2003, Hilton Atlanta, Atlanta, Georgia, p. 12.

32 Wayne Grudem, "Should We Move Beyond the New Testament to a Better Ethic? An Analysis of William J. Webb, *Slaves, Women and Homosexuals: Exploring the Hermeneutics of Cultural Analysis*," Journal of the Evangelical Theological Society 47, no. 2 (June 2004), p. 346.

CHAPTER THREE

William J. Webb's book

Along with the response of local pastors and the USA interlocuters like Schreiner, Grudem, and MacDonald, a letter was sent to the Board of Directors on September 14, 2004. This letter asked the school to create a doctrinal task force to evaluate if Webb's book was in contradiction to the school's stance on the Bible as the final authority.[33] The Doctrinal Examination Committee was thus created. The conclusion of the committee's findings was presented in April 2005 where it was announced that the RMH "does not deny, explicitly or implicitly, the inerrancy or final authority of the Bible." This report

---

33 Letter to Chairman, September 14, 2004 (Board Doctrinal Committee File, Box: President Brubacher Archive 1).

was then affirmed by the board on May 30, 2005.[34] The school thus continued to be open to the use of the RMH and continued to allow for the position of both complementarianism and egalitarianism.

This decision of the doctrinal task force was made shortly after FEBC churches voted against having practicing egalitarian churches within its ranks. This decision only came about after much discussion and deliberation. The vote to pass this bylaw took place at the national convention on November 1–3, 2004. 404 ballots were cast, with 299 voting in favour of not having egalitarian churches within their midst and 103 against.[35] Thus, with the motion carried at the FEBC and the school continuing to allow for both positions, there was an obvious friction between some FEBC leaders and the school.

The turning point

The 2000–2001 and 2001–2002 school years brought further challenges. In Brubacher's 2002 report, he took note of the way that "events and trends such as September 11, the plunging stock market, the low interest rate, the threat of terrorism, the collapse of major corporations, the dialogue about women in church leadership … all had a stressful impact on Heritage." Adding to all of this stress was a deficit in the 2000–2001 and the 2001–2002 school years.[36] By contrast, both the 2002–2003 and the 2003–2004 school years ended with a surplus.[37] From 2004 onward, however, the school faced grow-

---

34 "A statement from the board of directors of Heritage College & Seminary Concerning a 'Redemptive-Movement Hermeneutic,' May 31, 2005," p. 1 (Board Doctrinal Committee File).

35 I am thankful to Steven Jones, President of the FEBC, for this information. Steven Jones, Email to Jonathan N. Cleland, August 22, 2023. Also on this convention, see Marg Buchanan, "Pastoral role open to men only," *Christian Week*, (November 26, 2004) (https://www.christianweek.org/pastoral-role-open-to-men-only; accessed August 22, 2023).

36 "President's Annual Report, Presented to the Board of Directors at the Annual Celebration, September 24, 2002," pp. 1, 3 (President's Annual Reports [Annual Meetings] File).

37 "President's Annual Report, Presented to the Board of Directors at the Annual Celebration, September 22, 2003," p. 4 (President's Annual Reports [Annual Meetings] File) and "President's Annu-

CHAPTER THREE

ing difficulties. After the 2004–2005 school year there was a $23,935 deficit.[38] The following school year saw another deficit of $220,759.[39] In Brubacher's September 2007 annual report, he noted "a third year of declining enrollment and a significant budget deficit."[40] In 2004 there were 253 students enrolled in the College. By 2005 there were 224 students; 2006 there were 211; and by 2007 there were 194—part of the challenge being the loss of ten students through the closing of the Bachelor of Christian Student Education (BCSE) program. Similar to the college, the seminary also saw a decrease in enrollment, with only 18 new students in 2007 compared to 33 new students in 2005.[41]

This decrease in enrollment also exacerbated the ongoing financial issues, as the school ended the 2006–2007 school year "with an operating deficit of $469,250."[42] To alleviate this financial situation, the school took out a loan in 2006 and requested another in 2007 in order to pay for operating costs.[43] When the board of directors met to address the question of Heritage's future in October 2007, they saw only two options. First, Heritage could merge with another Canadian

---

al Report, Presented to the Board of Directors at the Annual Celebration, September 27, 2004," p. 3 (President's Annual Reports [Annual Meetings] File).

38 "President's Annual Report, Presented to the Board of Directors at the Annual Celebration, September 26, 2005," p. 3 (President's Annual Reports [Annual Meetings] File).

39 "President's Annual Report, Presented to the Board of Directors at the Annual Meeting, September 25, 2006," pp. 1, 3 (President's Annual Reports [Annual Meetings] File).

40 "President's Annual Report, Presented to the Board of Directors at the Annual Meeting, September 24, 2007," p. 1 (Heritage Board of Directors Meetings Nov 2004– File, Box: President Brubacher Archive 2).

41 "President's Annual Report, Presented to the Board of Directors at the Annual Meeting, September 24, 2007," p. 3. Brubacher mentioned that at one point the BCSE program had 50 full-time students and therefore, the loss of this program was an important factor in the financial challenges. Marvin Brubacher, Email to Jonathan N. Cleland, August 24, 2023.

42 "President's Annual Report, Presented to the Board of Directors at the Annual Meeting, September 24, 2007," p. 3.

43 "Heritage College & Seminary, Report to FaithLife Financial, October 23, 2007," p. 1 (Heritage Board of Directors Meetings Nov 2004– File).

school, or second, they would either need to close part of the school (college or seminary) or shut down the school entirely.[44] At this meeting the board considered four schools with which a potential merger could take place: McMaster Divinity School, Trinity Western University, Tyndale University College & Seminary, or Briercrest College and Seminary.[45] A fifth school, Emmanuel Bible College in Kitchener, was also considered as a possible merger partner, although the leadership at Emmanuel had similar concerns about their decreased enrollment.[46]

No decision on a possible merger was forthcoming, though the financial situation of the school continued to worsen. In 2008, Brubacher's annual report mentioned a $628,339 deficit.[47] In September 2009, Brubacher noted the way that the financial crisis of 2007–2008 had had an impact on Heritage and other Christian schools. The donation goal for that year was $1,177,300, but only $509,130 was received. Reflecting on this situation, Brubacher commented, "The almost overwhelming challenges of leading and administrating a school in 'crisis mode' continue to wear on me daily."[48]

Just a month prior, on August 5, 2009, the board had met on a conference call for a special meeting. Here, Brubacher presented the possibility of a merger with Emmanuel as the best option for the future survival of the school. The deficit for the year was $639,081

---

44 "Heritage Baptist College and Heritage Theological Seminary, Board of Directors' Meeting, Monday, October 29, 2007" (Heritage Board of Directors Meetings Nov 2004– File).

45 "Heritage Baptist College and Heritage Theological Seminary, Board of Directors' Meeting, Monday, October 29, 2007."

46 President and Board Chairman, Letter to Marvin Brubacher, November 19, 2007 (Heritage Board of Directors Meetings Nov 2004– File).

47 "Heritage College & Seminary Executive Committee/Board, President's Report and Evaluation, September 25, 2008," p. 1 (Heritage Executive Committee File, Box: President Brubacher Archive 2).

48 "Heritage College & Seminary Executive Committee/Board, President's Report and Evaluation, September 12, 2009," p. 1 (Heritage Executive Committee File).

CHAPTER THREE

and there was therefore a call to cut the budget by 20%. At this meeting, Brubacher stated that the only option was to either finalize the merger or close the school.[49] In the academic year of 2010–2011 everything came to a head. Although the financial situation was better than previous years, the 2009–2010 school year had still ended with a $243,086 deficit.[50] The continued year-end deficits highlighted the need for a restructuring and thus two of the faculty—one of whom was William Webb— did not have their employment renewed for the 2010–2011 school year.[51] With none of the mergers working and financial resources at their end, Brubacher decided to go to the FEBC to voice the school's desperate need for the denomination to intervene. The Baptist denomination agreed to step in, and the new board that was created had four members from Heritage and six from the FEBC. As it turned out, this new direction through the partnership of FEBC and Heritage brought Brubacher's time as president to a close. For a brief period of time, following the 2011 graduation, he served as the school's chancellor.[52]

There is no doubt that Marvin Brubacher was a key figure in the history of Heritage. He was an integral piece in the founding of LBBC/S, played a central role in the merger with CBS, and was the leading figure in Heritage's relocation from London to Cambridge. From 1990–2011, Brubacher served as a president—first at LBBC/S (1990–1993) and then at Heritage (1993–2011). One of the ways in which this vital ministry is still remembered at the school is through

---

49 "Minutes of Special Meeting of the Board of Directors, Wednesday, August 5, 2009, Conference Call," pp. 1–2 (Heritage Board of Directors Meetings Nov 2004– File).

50 "President's Annual Report, Presented to the Board of Directors at the Annual Meeting, September 27, 2010," p. 3 (Heritage Board of Directors File, Box: President Brubacher Archive 2).

51 "Minutes of the Special Meetings of the Board of Directors, Friday, February 19, 2010, Conference Call," pp. 1–2 (Heritage Board of Directors File).

52 Jonathan N. Cleland, "Zoom interview with Marvin Brubacher," April 14, 2023.

CHAPTER THREE

Marvin Brubacher

the Marvin Brubacher Citizenship Award—an award given "to the top non-graduating male student and one female student who have demonstrated godly character and have been extensively involved in student life at Heritage."[53]

Conscious that some of the decline in giving was linked to the school's openness to egalitarianism, after graduation 2011, the board started to require faculty members to be committed to complementarianism. This led to a number of faculty and staff leaving. While painful, this decision to be explicitly complementarian clarified the school's theological stance and better aligned Heritage with the conviction of the FEBC churches. Rather than seeking to merge with another school, Heritage sought to create a clearer confessional identity that made them unique. And as the next ten years revealed, this step

---

53 "Heritage 2023–2024 College Academic Catalogue," p. 22.

CHAPTER THREE

Rick and Linda Reed

proved to be an important turning point in the history of Heritage.

Now that Brubacher was no longer serving as the president, the school was faced with the task of finding a new leader. After a search process of roughly a year, this search culminated in the hiring of Rick Reed.

The leadership of Rick Reed
After being diagnosed with prostate cancer, Rick Reed went to Mt. Hermon Christian Conference Center in California in order to spend time praying about the next steps for his life. While he was there, on February 25, 2011, he prayed, and as he recalled, "the words 'Pastors' College' kept coming to my mind, along with a sense that I was to invest time and energy in training pastors, missionaries and church leaders." Later he wrote in his journal:

CHAPTER THREE

Felt the deep stirring of a calling to train pastors, leaders and missionaries. Drawn to the need in Canada but also more globally. The words 'pastors' college' came into my thinking. Not sure all that it means, but I returned with a sense of having a significant moment with God at Mt. Hermon.[54]

This calling was connected to another one that Reed had experienced over twenty-five years previously when he was lined up to go to Brazil to teach in a seminary. Due to certain circumstances, it never worked out. Nevertheless, following his trip to Mt. Hermon and his cancer treatment, his church, the Metropolitan Bible Church in Ottawa, allowed him to serve for a period overseas and to teach courses at Heritage. A year following his experience at Mt. Hermon, he received a phone call from one of the board members at Heritage. The board member asked Reed if he would consider being the next president.[55]

Reed had been the pastor at Metropolitan Bible Church in Ottawa since 1998. As a news article from February 2013 put it, Reed was a "well-loved pastor" and under his preaching, the church had grown from 800 to 2,400 people. However, due to Reed's desire to be more closely involved in the training of men and women for ministry, when he was approached to become the president, it clearly seemed to be a call from God. Reed resigned from his role at Metropolitan Bible Church on October 1, 2012, and started at Heritage as the president on January 1, 2013.[56] Mike Nichols, who was the board chair at the

---

54 Rick Reed, *A Priceless Heritage* (Cambridge, ON: Heritage College & Seminary, n.d.), pp. 2–3.
55 Reed, *A Priceless Heritage*, pp. 2–3.
56 Frank Stirk, "Well-loved pastor takes the reins at Heritage College and Seminary," *ChristianWeek* (February 26, 2013) (https://www.christianweek.org/well-loved-pastor-takes-the-reins-at-heritage-college-and-seminary/; accessed August 17, 2023).

time, made the following comment about the hiring of Reed: "It is with much gratitude to God that after conducting an extensive search Dr. Rick Reed has accepted the Board's offer to be the new President of Heritage. Dr. Reed is passionate about Heritage's mission to glorify God by training men and women for life and ministry."[57]

Sylvia Chin, who worked at Heritage Seminary as the executive assistant to the dean from July 2008 to November 2013, commented on how morale was quote low during the 2010–2012 period. There was a lack of clarity regarding the future and a fear that the school might be shutting down. However, this totally changed when Reed was hired in 2013. Chin commented that, under his leadership, there was a sense of passion and excitement in the school again. He was well received and soon began to attract new students and supporters.[58]

"Where would I be 10 years from now?"
Julia Rogler

In September 2012 I emptied the contents of my parents overpacked van into my dorm room, wondering, "where would I be 10 years from now?" I came to Heritage with no specific career expectations, just an interest in worshipping God through music. Over my five years in the Bachelor of Church Music program I learned more about God, his people, and how he desires us to worship him, but the most impactful things were experienced in relationships.

---

57 "Dr. Reed appointed president of Heritage College & Seminary," *Cision* (October 18, 2012), (https://www.newswire.ca/news-releases/dr-reed-appointed-president-of-heritage-college--seminary-510979121.html; accessed August 17, 2023).

58 Jonathan N. Cleland, "Interview with Sylvia Chin, Kitchener, Ontario, June 9, 2023."

CHAPTER THREE

> My favourite years were when I learned the value of needing godly people to shape and lead me by example. During my internship at Benton Street Baptist Church, I experienced the kindness and patience of Dr. Doug Thomson—also the Director of Music at Heritage. As I began applying my classroom knowledge and skills to the Sunday worship services, he graciously taught me by example how to lovingly lead others. He intentionally invested in me and modelled great leadership in such a way that ten years after that September move-in day I would find myself the director of Music and Worship at Benton Street Baptist Church. To this day, I'm so thankful to have the continued support of Doug and his wife.

Julia Rogler

Under Reed's direction, the school focused on a few key areas, two of which will be noted here. First, Reed looked to build closer partnerships with local churches. This was shown not only in the way that Heritage more than doubled the amount of partner churches over Reed's tenure, but also in the encouraging of local churches to be proactive in finding prospective students and sending them to Heritage for ministerial training. Second, Reed came to the school

CHAPTER THREE

A useful pastor

with a high view of expository preaching. An excellent preacher himself, Reed was involved in seeing many students trained to do expository preaching. As he himself has stated, "Pastors have to do more than preach well, but they can't do less."[59] In answering the question of what an effective minister should look like, Reed, while teaching a class on the Pastoral Epistles, drew the following image of what eighteenth-century Baptists called "a useful pastor."

As exemplified in this drawing, the leaders that Heritage sought to train are people who, first, stand on two legs: the one depending on a personal and robust relationship with Christ, and the other

---

59 Recordings by Rick Reed, received by Jonathan N. Cleland, May 23, 2023.

committed to an authentic and godly Christian character and life. Second, they are those who shepherd well, those who "love the sheep." Third, they are men who faithfully preach the Word of God. Fourth, they are leaders who have "the ability to lead wisely and well." And fifth, they have the ability to "see the mission." As Reed stated, "We want every student [to] be spiritually 'near-sighted' (seeing the needs of the lost people locally) and 'far-sighted' (seeing the needs of lost people globally)."[60]

"Deep and profound formation in the way of Jesus"
Alex Guenther

My overall experience as a student at Heritage has been one of deep and profound formation in the way of Jesus as I aim towards pastoral ministry. Heritage as a school seeks to speak to and educate the whole person; both mind and soul, head and heart. In my pursuit of my Bachelor of Theology, I was able to learn from professors who were knowledgeable and intelligent, unafraid to confront assumed positions and ideas with

Alex Guenther

---

60 Reed, *A Priceless Heritage*, pp. 8–9.

the truth of Scripture. However, both in the classroom and one-on-one, I was also able to experience the pastoral warmth of many of these professors who were seeking to not just fill their students' minds with truth, but to fill their students' hearts with love for God and others as they spoke the truth. Furthermore, being able to study and live life in a community of students that is open about their faith and is genuinely aiming to serve each other has been a great encouragement to my faith and calling. As I begin pursuing my M.Div, I am excited to see how God will use Heritage in my life to further shape me as a person into the image of Jesus.

"A rich education"
Parker Arnold

I am thankful that God blessed me with a rich education at Heritage Theological Seminary. I recall a very warm community of fellow learners, administrators, and professors that, as I later learned at another institution, was rare. There was a very clear sense that Heritage is a

Parker Arnold

place that study and faith are intertwined through the aims of preparing men and women for service of Christ, his Church, and his kingdom. This is evidenced by the many professors who have rich pastoral/ministerial experiences along with robust academic credentials. Their instruction has given me great clarity on my identity as a Christian and has helped me discern my place in God's mission. I can certainly say that my fogginess of both those elements would not have cleared if it were not for my education at Heritage. I praise God for that school and the men and women who have devoted seasons of their life to keeping it thrive.

"What Heritage has meant to me"
Roy M. Paul, ThD, FRHistS

My childhood ambition was to be a scientist. After a long career working in drug development for a major pharmaceutical company, I retired early. On my last day, as I went down the walkway to the parking lot I stopped, realizing that my career was finished. I had such a feeling of despondency and emptiness. I became involved in volunteer work; however, my wife knew I was restless. She suggested that since I loved to learn and teach, I should take a few Bible courses. I attended classes at Heritage one day, came home and announced I was going to do a Master's degree!

CHAPTER THREE

> Initially I was concerned that I would not be able to handle the work, having been out of school for over 40 years but the faculty assured me that they would support me in whatever was required for me to successfully complete my program. In 2016 I graduated with an MTS, and received the Academic Achievement Award for the highest marks.
>
>
> Roy M. Paul
>
> I went on to complete a Th.D. in Church History, in 2020. The programs at Heritage are perfectly balanced, to provide in depth studies of Scripture, Theology, Ethics, and Spirituality. My time at Heritage provided me with a new sense of purpose in life, and a second career, doing proofreading and editing for works in development for publication.

From 2013–2020, the school witnessed financial stability and overall growth in the student body. In particular, the student enrollment in the seminary grew. In the fall of 2010, there were 104 seminary students. By the fall of 2016 there were 175 and four years later there were 211. The overall enrollment increased as well, from 305 in the fall of 2010 to 360 in the fall of 2018. However, the college numbers decreased significantly from winter 2011 (180 students) to

CHAPTER THREE

The student body, 2017-2018

winter 2020 (147 students).[61]

Financially, the operating budget for each academic year from 2010–2011 to 2019–2020 ended in a surplus.[62] At one point, the school owed $3,700,000, and through generous donations, this was totally eliminated on October 1, 2019.[63]

In 2020, Heritage, along with other churches and schools around the world, was faced with the impact of the COVID-19 pandemic. Heritage looked to adapt by providing online classes, and this move accelerated the school's online presence, eventually enabling Heritage to offer in-person as well as synchronous and asynchronous online classes.

On October 1, 2021, the school started a capital campaign called "Heritage for Canada & the Nations." This campaign had three goals. First, to enlarge the school's campus, primarily through the construction of a dedicated seminary building that would "provide

---

61 Carolyn Burgess, Email to Jonathan N. Cleland, September 1, 2023.
62 Shawn Goble, Email to Jonathan N. Cleland, August 28, 2023.
63 Rick and Linda Reed, "Paid in Full!" (https://rickandlindareed.com/2019/10/01/paid-in-full/ ;accessed October 28, 2023).

CHAPTER THREE

Rick Reed

much needed space and raise the profile of the seminary within the Heritage community." Second, to "extend our training" by introducing new programs, offering more scholarships and options for distance learning, expanding the library, and supporting faculty and staff. And third, to "expand our impact," through ventures like a Global Outreach Centre and a dedicated Heritage Seminary Press.[64]

On August 16, 2023, an email was sent out announcing Reed's transition from his role as President to a new role as Chancellor.[65] This brings to end yet another era in the life of the school. Reed provided ten years of fruitful leadership at Heritage. Through him, the school saw an increase in partner churches and an increase in

---

64 "Heritage for Canada & The Nations" (https://heritageforcanada.ca; accessed Aug 20, 2023).
65 "Heritage College & Seminary—Leadership Update" Email, August 16, 2023.

students and financial support. He will be remembered for his excellent expository preaching, his personal and pastoral heart, and his desire to see men and women trained for faithful service to Christ and his Church here in Canada and around the world.

> ### "Heritage has been as a spiritual home to me"
> Sean Sheeran
>
>
>
> **Sean Sheeran & family**
>
> My first exposure to Heritage was not as a student but landscaping on campus as a very new Christian in 2003. I had been brought along by an elder at the church where I heard the gospel, who prayed with me when I received Christ, and who was discipling me while we worked together. I recall watching students go back and forth with wonder and amazement. Prior to this I was unaware Bible

> colleges even existed! This newfound prospect of studying God's Word quickly created an intense longing in me to become one of those students. Little did I know then how instrumental Heritage would be in my own life and future ministry. By God's grace I was vitally formed as a new believer while studying at the College. I would not be who I am today apart from conversations with fellow students, rich lectures from gifted and passionate professors, and the many fabulous resources put into my hands. Similarly, I would not have been equipped for pastoral ministry apart from the combined community of both College and Seminary. For almost 20 years, alongside my local church, Heritage has been as a spiritual home to me. Words fail to express the full extent of my gratitude for those special years, people, and place!

"An enterprise of faith"

September 2023 marks Heritage's 30th anniversary. It marks thirty years of God working through a Bible College and Seminary in Ontario that has equipped men and women to serve Christ and his Church locally, nationally, and globally. In his 1997 report, president Brubacher commented that the history of Heritage, up to that point, could be described as "an enterprise of faith." What he then wrote about the conclusion of the 1996–1997 school year can be seen as an accurate comment about the entire history of Heritage so far. As Brubacher went on to state, "At the conclusion of another year of Heritage … let us praise God for what He has accomplished in and through this ministry as we have walked by faith together."[66] Similarly, as Theresa Beach commented on her over twenty years at Heritage, both as a student and as a member of staff, she recounted the many friends and colleagues she has seen be used by God in continual and faithful ministry. Reflecting on the impact Heritage has had, she stated, "This is God's work … the hand of God, using Heritage, over and over."[67]

At the end of thirty years we, along with the Psalmist, rightly say together:

> Not to us, LORD, not to us
> but to your name be the glory,
> because of your love and faithfulness.[68]

Soli Deo Gloria.

---

[66] "President's Annual Report, Presented to the Board of Directors at the Annual Celebration, September 27, 1997," p. 1.
[67] Cleland, "Zoom interview with Beach," May 9, 2023.
[68] Psalm 115:1, NIV.

www.ingramcontent.com/pod-product-compliance
Lightning Source LLC
Chambersburg PA
CBHW070951080526
44587CB00015B/2260